DISASTER
GREAT LAKES

Thunder Bay Press

Copyright © 2002 by Lynx Images Inc.
P.O. Box 5961, Station A
Toronto, Canada M5W 1P4
Web Site: http://www.lynximages.com

Exclusively distributed in the United States by

Holt, Michigan

1st Edition: May 2002

Project Producers: Russell Floren, Barbara Chisholm and Andrea Gutsche
Cover and inside design: Andrea Gutsche, Lynx Images Inc.

Front Cover: The Great Fire at Chicago, October 8th, 1871, Currier & Ives
—Chicago Historical Society

Back Cover Main: *Phoenix* burns off Sheboygan, WI, 1847.
—Wisconsin Maritime Museum

Inset Left: Foundering of the *Edmund Fitzgerald*, 1975 by artist David Conklin.
—Commissioned by the Great Lakes Shipwreck Historical Society. Prints available from: Shipwreck Coast Museum Store, Whitefish Point, Michigan (Large (17"x22") and small (8.5" x 11") Call 906-492-3747 or www.shipwreckmusem

Inset Right: Fleeing to the Peshtigo River, 1871. Many drowned in the river or were injured by flying debris. Some reports estimate that as many as 1200 people were killed in Peshtigo, Wisconsin and surrounding areas.
—Wisconsin Historical Society (Iconographic Collection)

National Library of Canada Cataloguing in Publication Data
Long, Megan, 1975-
    Disaster Great Lakes

Includes bibliographical references and index.
ISBN 1-882376-88-9

1. Disaster—Great Lakes—Regionl History. I. Title.

F551.L66 2002   977   C2022-900630-9

DISASTER
GREAT LAKES

By Megan Long

CONTENTS

FLEEING TO THE PESHTIGO RIVER, 1871

In October 1871 people ran for the safety of the Pestigo River as fire devastated Peshtigo, Wisconsin, leaving about 1,200 people dead. The Canadian Great Lakes region has also been stricken by fire. One of the worst was the Mississagi fire of 1948 (along the North Channel leading to Lake Superior). No cause was ever found for the fire that burned for two months, razing 1,000 square miles. More timber was burned than was cut in 50 years of logging.

INTRODUCTION

A journey from the open water of Lake Superior to the crowded shipping channels of Lake Ontario, *Disaster Great Lakes* explores the history of disasters on and around these magnificent inland seas, from 1780 to the present.

Over the years, the Great Lakes have been full of activity. Battles were fought for control of their shores and waters, and thousands of immigrants boarded ships and trains to head west to the promise of new and better lives. Boundless stands of timber, seemingly endless sources of mineral-rich ore and plentiful farmlands supported the growing population but, these bounties did not come without a price. The rugged shores of the Great Lakes can be unforgiving, and each year, unpredictable weather plagues the Lakes—with dire consequences.

During the 1800s the volume of shipping on and around the Great Lakes rose dramatically. Steamships carried immigrants and their belongings to new settlements. Booming commerce brought a huge increase in the shipment of goods. Railways spread along the shores and cities sprang to life.

With this increased traffic, it was inevitable that disasters would occur. Canada and the United States were young countries and laws governing transportation were almost non-existent. Railway tracks were laid in a hurry, and ships were compromised by overcrowding. With no lifejackets, too few lifeboats and no radios to send out distress calls, thousands of lives were lost when overloaded ships sank.

Fire was also a constant in people's lives. The lumber industry was booming and in 1871 and 1881 horrific forest fires swept through Wisconsin and Michigan—the result of poor lumber

HUMAN ERROR–*EASTLAND* CAPSIZED

More than 800 people drowned when the steamer Eastland *capsized in Chicago Harbor in July 1915.*
Authorities ignored several warnings about the dangerous list of the Eastland *and certified the vessel for*
more than 2500 passengers. As was the case with all steamers from the era, the number of passengers
far outnumbered the spaces available in lifeboats on board. Marine historians estimate that 4000 ships
have been lost on the Great Lakes due to storms, collisions, fires and scuttling.

practices. Fires would also devastate Chicago, the largest city on the Lakes. The Great Chicago Fire of 1871, fuelled by a concentration of wooden buildings, leveled the city core. Toronto suffered a similar fate in 1904.

As the Great Lakes region progressed into the 1900s there was a marked improvement in technology and safety regulations. Yet despite improvements in navigation and building techniques, these inland seas retained their power to wreak havoc. In 1940 an Armistice Day storm took 59 lives and in 1975 one of the largest and most modern ships on the Lakes, the *Edmund Fitzgerald*, disappeared from the radar screens on a stormy November night. Tough lessons too often were learned at great human cost. In 1929 the improper storage of a flammable material, x-ray film, caused a cloud of toxic gas at the Cleveland Clinic. The same city was rocked again in 1944 when a gas tank exploded at the East Ohio Gas Company.

During the latter part of the twentieth century, air travel increased rapidly in the Great Lakes region, bringing with it new disasters. These often provided the catalyst for improvements in technology. And in 1978 a hard but crucial lesson about polluting the land and water with toxins was learned as a result of the Love Canal crisis in Niagara Falls.

Disaster Great Lakes is filled with compelling stories that illuminate some of those particular moments in time that captivated nations. These events provide important insights into the past—the technological failings and resulting improvements, the laws that governed industries, and the people who traveled and worked on these magnificent lakes.

STORM OF 1905

(Top) Like so many of the worst storms on the Great Lakes, this one came in November. After three days of extreme weather, 14 vessels foundered leaving wreckage strewn around Lake Superior. The Monkshaven *struck Angus Island.*

THE HUMAN COST

(Below) The Iroquois Theater in Chicago was a brand new "absolutely fireproof" building in 1903 when a stage fire burned out of control and 601 people died. Penciling over images (as seen below) was commonly done to protect people's identities. Only 32 years earlier a booming Chicago was destroyed by the Great Fire of 1871, killing nearly 300 and leaving 100,000 homeless. In the same year massive timber fires in Michigan and Wisconsin took more than 1400 lives.

GREAT LAKES DISASTERS

1 Royal Navy sloop *Ontario* lost, near Wilson, New York, Nov. 1, 1780. Deaths: about 115
2 *Erie* burns off Silver Creek, New York, August 9, 1841. Deaths: 175-250
3 Hurricane-force winds, Lake Ontario and Lake Erie, 1844. Deaths: 200
4 Fire aboard the *Phoenix*, off Sheboygan, Wisconsin, November 21, 1847. Deaths: 200+
5 *G.P. Griffith* fire, off Willoughby Township, Ohio, June 16-17, 1850. Deaths: 250-300
6 *Atlantic* and *Ogdensburgh* collide, Long Point, Ontario, August 20, 1852. Deaths: 130-250
7 *Ocean Wave* burned off Duck Islands, Lake Ontario, April 30, 1853. Deaths: 33
8 *Conductor* founders off Long Point, Ontario, November 24, 1854. Deaths: 0
9 *Niagara* burned, near Sheboygan, Wisconsin, September 24, 1856. Deaths: 50-170
10 *Toledo* wrecked, off Port Washington, Wisconsin, October 22, 1856. Deaths: 40-55
11 *Superior* wrecked, near Pictured Rocks, Michigan, October 30, 1856. Deaths: 35
12 *Lady Elgin* sinks off Winnetka, Illinois, September 8, 1860. Deaths: 297
13 *Keystone State* foundered, off Port Austin, Michigan, November 10, 1861. Deaths: 33
14 *Pewabic* collides with *Meteor*, off Alpena, Michigan, August 9, 1865. Deaths: 75-125
15 *Seabird* burned, off Waukegan, Illinois, April 9, 1868. Deaths: 102
16 *R.G. Coburn* lost near Presque Isle, Michigan, October 14, 1871. Deaths: 32
17 Great Fire of Peshtigo, Wisconsin, October 8, 1871. Deaths: 1200
18 Great Chicago Fire, October 8, 1871. Deaths: about 300
19 Michigan Timber Fires, October 1871, September 1881. Deaths: about 500
20 *Galena* wreck, off Thunder Bay, Ontario, September 24, 1872. Deaths: unknown
21 Ashtabula Bridge Collapse, Ashtabula, Ohio, Christmas 1876. Deaths: 156
22 *Jane Miller* sinks, off Colpoy's Bay, Ontario, November 26, 1881. Deaths: 30
23 Sinking of the *Asia*, Georgian Bay, Ontario, September 14, 1882. Deaths: 120
24 *Algoma* wreck, Isle Royale, Lake Superior, November 7, 1885. Deaths: 31-48
25 *Chicora* foundered, between Milwaukee, WI, and St. Joseph, MI, January 21, 1895. Deaths: 25
26 Osceola Mine Shaft #3 Fire, near Calumet, Michigan, September 7, 1895. Deaths: 30
27 Galveston Hurricane, Great Lakes Basin, September 11, 1900. Deaths: 11
28 Loss of the *Bannockburn*, Lake Superior, November 22, 1902. Deaths: 21
29 Iroquois Theater Fire, Chicago, Illinois, December 30, 1903. Deaths: 601
30 Great Lakes Gales, 1905. Deaths: 116
31 *Mataafa* foundered, Duluth, Minnesota, November 28, 1905. Deaths: 9
32 Collinwood School Fire, Cleveland, Ohio, March 4, 1908. Deaths: 174
33 *Marquette & Bessemer No. 2* sinks between Conneaut, Ohio, and Port Stanley, Ontario, December 7-8, 1909. Deaths: 31
34 Spanish River Train Derailment, Webbwood, Ontario, January 21, 1910. Deaths: 43

> Upon the chaos dark and rude
> And bid its angry tumult cease
> And give, for wild confusion, peace
> Oh, hear us when we cry to Thee
> for those in peril on the sea!
> —Mariner's Hymn

35 *Hamilton* and *Scourge* sink, mouth of Niagara River, August 8, 1913. Deaths: about 100

36 Red Jacket Hoax, Calumet, Michigan, December 24, 1913. Deaths: 76

37 Great Lakes Gales, November 7-10, 1913. Deaths: 235

38 Capsizing of *Eastland*, Chicago, Illinois, July 24, 1915. Deaths: 835-844

39 Detroit Streetcar Collision, April 15, 1915. Deaths: 15

40 Flood, Erie, Pennsylvania, August 3, 1915. Deaths: 26

41 *James B. Colgate* lost, off Long Point, Ontario, October 20, 1916. Deaths: 25

42 Cloquet-Moose Lake Fire, Minnesota, October 12, 1918. Deaths: 800

43 *Superior City* collided with *Willis L. King*, Whitefish Bay, Lake Superior, August 20, 1920. Deaths: 29

44 *Clifton* lost, northwest of Oscoda, Michigan, September 22, 1924. Deaths: 27

45 Barnes-Hecker Iron Mine Cave-In, Michigan, November 3, 1926. Deaths: 51

46 Cleveland, Ohio, Clinic Fire, May 15, 1929. Deaths: 123

47 Disappearance of the *Andaste*, between Grand Haven, Michigan, and Chicago, Illinois, September 9, 1929. Deaths: 25

48 Honeymoon Bridge Collapse, Niagara Falls, Ontario, and Niagara Falls, New York, January 27, 1938. Deaths: 0

49 Armistice Day Storm, Great Lakes, November 11, 1940: Deaths: 49 in Minnesota, 13 in Illinois, 4 in Michigan and 59 sailors in shipwrecks

50 East Ohio Gas Company Explosion, Cleveland, Ohio, October 20, 1944. Deaths: 130

51 *Noronic* Fire, Toronto, Ontario, September 17, 1949. Deaths: 119

52 Hurricane Hazel, Toronto, Ontario, October 15, 1954. Deaths: 81

53 *Carl D. Bradley* lost, near Gull Island, Michigan, November 18, 1958. Deaths: 33

54 Metropolitan Store Explosion, Windsor, Ontario, October 25, 1960. Deaths: 10

55 Tornado, Illinois, Ohio, Michigan, Wisconsin, April 11, 1965. Deaths: 116

56 *Daniel J. Morrell* sinks, north of Point Aux Barques, MI, November 29, 1966. Deaths: 28

57 Air Canada DC-8-63 Crashes at Toronto Airport, Ontario, July 5, 1970. Deaths: 109

58 Detroit Metropolitan Water System Tunnel Explosion, Port Huron, Michigan, December 11, 1971. Deaths: 21

59 *Edmund Fitzgerald* foundered, off Whitefish Point, MI, November 10, 1975. Deaths: 29

60 Love Canal Pollution, Niagara Falls, NY, First Evacuations August 1978. Deaths: unknown

61 Mississauga Train Disaster, Mississauga, Ontario, November 10, 1979. Deaths: 0

62 Mississauga Nursing Home Fire, Mississauga, Ontario, July 14, 1980. Deaths: 21

63 American Airlines Crash at Chicago, Illinois, O'Hare International Airport, May 25, 1979. Deaths: 273

*Events chosen for this list include disasters of historical significance in the Great Lakes region; some involved hundreds of deaths and some no deaths at all. Many are important because they brought on changes to their respective industries, or caused great disruption and expense. Others are included because they bring to light the heroism of individuals.

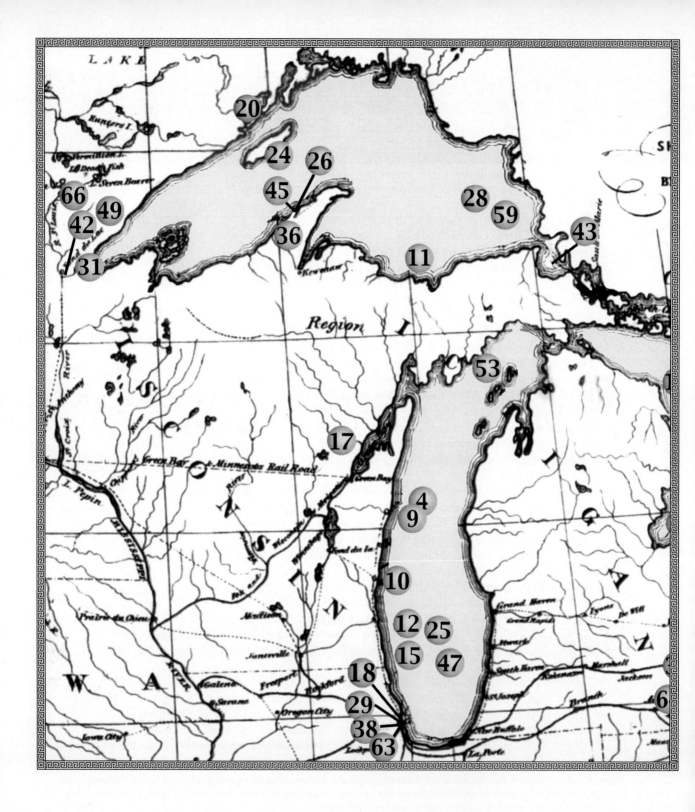

BETWEEN THE ATLANTIC SEABORD

AND THE

Great West.

Numbers on map correspond to the list of disasters on pp. x-xi.

LAKE SUPERIOR

FIRE RELIEF
Refugees from the Cloquet-Moose Lake fire line up to receive donations of clothing and medical treatment from the Red Cross and the Home Guard at the Duluth Armory.

PRIDE OF CANADIAN PACIFIC RAILWAY

The CPR's 262-foot (79m) liner Algoma is pictured before the wreck of November 7, 1885. The Algoma was one of three liners built for the CPR in Scotland.

WRECKED ON GREENSTONE ISLAND

(Bottom) The Algoma was repeatedly smashed onto the rocks of Greenstone Island, breaking it in two and scattering pieces of the hull along the shoreline.

GREENSTONE ISLAND TODAY

(Inset) Image from the documentary film Mysterious Islands which featured the Algoma tragedy. Rusting metal and other debris are visible today.

WRECK OF THE *ALGOMA*

Foundered At Isle Royale

NOVEMBER 7, 1885

The *Algoma* was one of three steel passenger and freight liners built in 1883 under the direction of Henry Beatty, general manager of Canadian Pacific's marine operations. The vessels (all with Canadian names), the *Algoma*, *Alberta*, and *Athabasca*, each 262 feet (79m) long and equipped with 130 first-class cabins and bunks for two hundred steerage passengers, crossed the Atlantic from Scotland to Montreal. Here they were cut in two to allow them to pass through the locks of the St. Lawrence River and the Welland Canal on their way to Port Colborne on Lake Erie. In the spring of 1884 they were put into service running from Owen Sound on Georgian Bay to Port Arthur at the head of Lake Superior.

Late in its second season, on Friday, November 6, the *Algoma* left the Sault canal and entered Lake Superior under the confident direction of Captain Moore. All day and into the night the *Algoma* raced along, both engines steaming, her sails drawing in the wind.

However, by 4 a.m. Saturday, the *Algoma* was pitching and rolling in a ferocious gale. Rain, sleet and snow pounded the ship and the captain had no choice but to turn the liner into the open lake until visibility improved. As the steamer swung around there was a bone-chilling crash of steel on rock. With its rudder smashed, the boat careened out of control. Like a toy, the *Algoma* was lifted by the huge waves and repeatedly dropped on the rocks of Greenstone Island just off Isle Royale. At 6 a.m. the ship broke in two and the bow disappeared into the black water. On the canted after-deck, the remaining passengers and crew clung desperately to a single lifeline.

As day broke, three brave crewmembers made the 60-foot (18m) swim to shore, but they could not find a way to ferry those left onboard. By Sunday morning the gale had abated enough to let the remaining survivors make their way to shore on a small raft. Of 45 passengers and crew only 14 survived. They were found by local fishermen and on Monday morning they were able to intercept the *Algoma's* sister ship, the *Athabasca*, to give them the tragic news.

AFTERMATH

Fourteen survivors were taken off Greenstone Island by the crew of the Athabasca, *a sister ship to the* Algoma.

MYSTERIOUS DISAPPEARANCE

The 245-foot (73.5m) canal steamer Bannockburn *is pictured before the vessel vanished on November 21, 1902. The vessel has never been found.*

GREAT LAKES' "FLYING DUTCHMAN"

Steamer *Bannockburn* Vanishes

NOVEMBER 21, 1902

Captain McMaugh of the steamer *Algonquin* may have been the last person to set eyes on the distinctive profile of the 245-foot (73.5m) canal steamer *Bannockburn*, with its three raking masts and tall funnel. Laden with 85,000 bushels of wheat, the steamer was downbound from Port Arthur, Ontario, heading for Midland, Ontario, and fighting a strong headwind. According to McMaugh, the *Bannockburn* was running well, but when he looked up a few moments later, he was surprised that the vessel was already out of sight.

Later that night, the steady wind became a full-blown gale and ships out on Lake Superior struggled to make headway. Days passed and the *Bannockburn* failed to reach the Sault locks. Although the vessel was posted as overdue, there was little concern. Most people hypothesized that the captain had taken shelter on the north shore of the lake and would turn up eventually.

By November 27, six days after leaving Port Arthur, it became obvious that the *Bannockburn* was missing. Differing newspaper accounts and telegrams caused a great deal of confusion and speculation. Some believed that the vessel was wrecked off Stannard Rock, where the steamer *John D. Rockefeller* had passed through a wreckage field. Captain McMaugh advanced the theory that the sudden, mysterious disappearance of the vessel was a result of the ship's boilers blowing up and causing the vessel to sink almost immediately. At the time, the only wreckage positively identified was a life jacket bearing the name *Bannockburn*, found on the beach near Marais, Michigan. The strings were tied, suggesting that it had slipped from a body.

Captain George R. Wood and his entire crew of twenty perished.

The wreck of the *Bannockburn* has never been located, but the vessel is rumored to live on in the form of a ghost ship—likening it to the legendary *Flying Dutchman*, which was wrecked off the Cape of Good Hope and is said to reappear from time to time as a phantom ship. Only a few years after the Bannockburn disappeared, sailors began to report the ghostly figure of the steamer sailing past Caribou Island, still trying to reach Sault Ste. Marie.

GHOST SHIP
The Bannockburn is often called the "Flying Dutchman" after the famous ghost ship that is said to appear off the Cape of Good Hope.

TAKING A POUNDING
Water streams over the deck of the Mataafa as the steamer battles pounding waves.

THE *MATAAFA* BLOW

Lake Michigan

NOVEMBER 28, 1905

On the morning of November 27, 1905, storm flags were hoisted at Duluth, Minnesota, although the day had dawned promisingly clear and crisp. It was not uncommon for storm flags to be posted in November but too often captains ignored them in favor of delivering their cargo on time. And so the steamers *Mataafa*, *Ira H. Owen*, *Harold B. Nye*, and *Isaac L. Ellwood* all left on that fateful day despite the warning.

The steel bulk freight steamer *Mataafa*, loaded with iron ore and towing the barge *James Nasmyth*, cleared the harbor at about 3:30 p.m. Four hours later the boat ran headlong into one of the worst storms of the season. Driven by 60 mph (96kph) winds, snow and spray swirled around the pilothouse, cutting visibility to almost zero. Even with a powerful 1400 horsepower engine, the *Mataafa* was making virtually no headway.

By 4 a.m., Captain R.F. Humble had had enough. He turned the *Mataafa* around and inched his way southwest, heading cautiously back to Duluth where over the past twelve hours winds were said to have been a steady 60 mph with gusts to 70 mph (112kph).

Shortly after noon on the 28th, Captain Richard England was nearing the entrance to the harbor, struggling to keep his 363-foot (109m) steamer, the *R. W. England*, on course. The entrance to Duluth is a narrow canal and no doubt Captain England was nervous about making it through without incident. As the boat neared the canal, England panicked and made a last-minute turn away, but in turning, the *England* became trapped in a trough of boiling seas and was pushed sideways, finally ending up on the shore near Superior, Wisconsin. Duluth harbor had claimed its first victim of the day.

Soon after, the *Isaac L. Ellwood* appeared off Duluth. Under Captain Cummings it had been bound for Two Harbors, Minnesota, and had taken a severe thrashing overnight. Crushing waves had shredded the tarpaulins on deck and loosened hatch covers, leaving the *Ellwood* susceptible to taking on water. The captain had wisely decided to turn around and make a run for Duluth.

Nearing the canal, the captain lined up the vessel and plowed ahead. As the crew held their breath, the boat strove to stay on course but the seas fought back. A massive wave lifted the *Ellwood* and smashed it against the south pier, puncturing several plates on the port side. Despite taking on water the boat managed to limp into the inner harbor, and was pushed by tugs into the shallows where the vessel settled to the bottom. Count two for the harbor.

By this time crowds had assembled on the piers to witness the unfolding drama. They were not to be disappointed. Just after 2 p.m., the *Mataafa* showed up. Two miles back it had dropped the *Nasmyth*, which waited out the storm at anchor. Nearing Duluth, Captain Humble ordered "full speed ahead" and pointed the bow towards the narrow entrance. Humble knew that he would have to be going as fast as possible to maintain maneuverability in the pitching seas. As the freighter approached the entrance at full speed, the crowd held its breath. At the moment when the *Mataafa* came abreast of the piers marking the entrance, a wave lifted the stern, momentarily driving the bow into the bottom. The stern, still with its forward momentum, slingshotted to port then crashed back into the water. The *Mataafa* drove straight into the

RESCUED AFTER A HARROWING NIGHT

The storm pounded the wrecked Mataafa *throughout the night. The Duluth lifesaving crew had to wait until morning to rescue the 15 survivors.*

north pier. The bow rebounded but the stern was tossed to starboard where it collided with the pier. The engine began to run furiously because the propeller had been sheared off, leaving the *Mataafa* completely at the mercy of the churning canal. The freighter was pushed back out into the open water and waves drove the helpless vessel onto the rocky shallows about 600 feet (180m) from shore.

Within minutes waves broke over the decks and tore away two lifeboats and a life raft, leaving the crew stranded. Water flooded in to the stern from an open gangway on the starboard side and with each new wave the stern sank lower in the water. Twelve crewmembers were driven onto the spar deck where they hid behind the smokestack and ventilators, trying to avoid being swept away. The second mate and three others finally decided to make a run for the relative safety of the forward cabin. Clinging to hatch covers in between each new onslaught of waves, three succeeded but the other was turned back.

About 4 p.m. a loud crack echoed from the ship as the *Mataafa* broke in two midway along the deck. With the stern sinking ever lower, the captain shouted through his megaphone to those onshore, pleading for help. But the crowd could do nothing except watch in horror as the drama unfolded in front of them. Crew from the Duluth lifesaving station, who would normally have been on the scene within minutes, were already occupied with saving those aboard the *England* and did not return to Duluth until 5 p.m. Though tired and numb they immediately set out to

TWO PIECES
The Mataafa *broke into two pieces during the storm. The city of Duluth can be seen in the background.*

11

DAMAGE UP CLOSE
(Left) The Mataafa's *ice-covered wheelhouse with all its windows blown out, before salvage began. (Below) The mangled propeller of the* Mataafa.

assist the *Mataafa*. Because it was futile to launch their lifeboat in the roiling water, they set up a Lyle gun and began to fire a line out to the *Mataafa* so they could rig a breeches buoy to take the crew off. Their attempts were futile. Some lines fell on the water-swept deck out of reach of the crew. Others snapped in the cold. Still others met their mark but the captain and his crew were too exhausted to rig the buoy. Soon after midnight the lifesavers made the decision to wait until the seas calmed in order to rescue the crew by lifeboat.

On board the *Mataafa* there were fifteen men crowded into the captain's forward cabin with kerosene lamps as their only heat source. Throughout the night they tried to keep warm by moving constantly. At 5 a.m. the last lamp burned out but Captain Humble was determined to keep all of the men alive and so he made his way through the flooded passageways searching out more kerosene, some rags and dry matches. With a fire ax, he attacked the bathroom walls, breaking them up for firewood with which he built a fire in a bathtub he had dragged into the windlass room.

On shore an estimated ten thousand Duluth residents built bonfires and watched over the *Mataafa* through the long night. Finally, near 7:30 a.m., egged on by the cheers of the crowd, the lifesavers twice rowed out to the wreck and ferried survivors to safety. The third trip was not as triumphant. A news reporter described the scene: "A glance at the stern of the sunken boat told only too plainly the sad story of those unfortunates who were imprisoned in that part of the vessel by raging waves." The rescuers knew that nine men had been trapped there but they found only four bodies covered in ice and frozen to the vessel. The rest were presumed lost to the waves.

SALVAGE BEGINS

The Mataafa was salvaged in June 1906 by the company Reids of Sarnia and rebuilt the following year. The vessel went on to another 60 years on the lakes.

ON STRIKE!

Miners demonstrate on the streets of Calumet, Michigan, in 1913. The left placard shows a picture of James MacNaughton, general manager of the Calumet and Hecla Mining Company, and refers to the gunfire that rang out over the closed mine shafts (inset) where skirmishes between striking workers and mine security broke out and two striking miners were killed.

RED JACKET HOAX

Calumet, Michigan

DECEMBER 24, 1913

The winter of 1913 was particularly difficult for the mineworkers of northwestern Michigan. Those at Calumet and surrounding areas had been on strike since July 23 of that year. Money was short and tempers shorter. Fighting between mine security and striking workers had broken out on several occasions and the mining towns were being torn apart by the tension.

Nevertheless, the women in the community were determined not to let tight budgets and ill feeling spoil Christmas. They organized a Christmas Eve party for area miners and their families at Red Jacket's Italian Hall in Calumet.

The strike was forgotten as they climbed the stairs to the hall, excited children leaping them two by two. The air was filled with excitement in anticipation of the appearance of Kris Kringle, who would give out presents. A hush fell over the crowd. Suddenly a cry of "fire!" shattered the silence.

The crowd panicked and ran in a wave towards the stairs that led to the exit, knocking over chairs and pushing each other in their terror. The first to reach the top of the stairs fell headlong, propelled by the weight of the people behind. More and more bodies crashed down and heaped together at the bottom in a flailing mass of arms, legs and torsos.

By the time the panic subsided, 76 people, including 56 children, had been lost—senselessly, as it turned out, because there had been no fire in Red Jacket's that afternoon.

A Woody Guthrie ballad blames the "copper boss thugs" for the hoax but the coroner's jury returned an open verdict, stating that the mining companies could not be blamed.

COPPER MINERS
Mineworkers were determined their families would enjoy the Christmas party, in spite of the tensions caused by the five-month-long strike.

Carlton County Vidette.

VOLUME NO. XXXI.   THE CARLTON COUNTY VIDETTE, CARLTON, CARLTON COUNTY, MINNESOTA.   FRIDAY, OCTOBER 18, 1918.   NUMBER 48.

AWFULLEST FIRE HORROR IN STATE'S HISTORY!
Probably 900 Lives Gone! Property Loss Also Terrible!

HORROR

(Above) This local news headline tells the story of the Cloquet-Moose Lake fire, which was overshadowed in the national newspapers by the First World War.

ROOT CELLAR COFFIN

(Middle) Many families took refuge in their root cellars but were suffocated when the fire swept over their land. This man is digging bodies out of a root cellar.

AFTERMATH

(Lower) The burned ruins of the Duluth and Northeastern Railroad roundhouse in Cloquet, Minnesota. Relief trains saved thousands of people fleeing their burning towns, but the railroad companies were accused of starting the devastating fires.

16

THE CLOQUET-MOOSE LAKE FIRE

Northeastern Minnesota

OCTOBER 12, 1918

The summer of 1918 had been particularly dry in northeastern Minnesota and hundreds of small fires had been smoldering in the area's forests and peat bogs. On the afternoon of October 12, 1918, the humidity level in the region dropped drastically, and a 60-mph (96kph) wind ripped through the area, igniting dormant embers in the underbrush. The embers grew into flames and several fires swept across the region.

The Cloquet and Moose Lake regions were hit the hardest. At Cloquet, thousands crowded onto trains trying to escape. "The trains pulled out with the fires blazing closely behind them.... The flames licked at the cars. Windows in the coaches were broken by the heat." Thankfully most succeeded, but it was a different story in the Moose Lake region. A relief train requested at 3 p.m. was not sent out from Moose Lake by the Soo Line until 6 p.m. Its route was to take it to Kettle River, Automba, and Lawler but on arrival in Kettle River it was stopped by the advancing fire.

Those fleeing the area in cars had to negotiate the crowded, narrow road to Moose Lake. They were often blinded by smoke. Many were killed when they ran off the road into ditches. Many more died in root cellars, suffocated by smoke as the flames raced across their farms. In all, conservative estimates placed the death toll at 800.

Before the day was over, 1500 square miles (3900km^2) were destroyed, from the slopes of the Mesaba Range northwest of Duluth, southeast to Two Harbors, Minnesota. Public opinion placed blame with the railroad companies. With three major lines crisscrossing the region, fires were a common occurrence ignited by sparks and embers blowing from the smokestacks.

FIRE SCENE IN MOOSE L

BURNED

This photograph shows young Aina Jokimaki Johnson with bandaged hands and legs. The fire destroyed 26 settlements, leaving 13,000 homeless.

How Could it Happen?

The foundering of the Edmund Fitzgerald was a shock to the Great Lakes shipping industry. When the freighter was launched in 1958 it was the largest on the lakes. Ship-watchers, painters and photographers often chose this "Queen of the Lakes" as their subject.

THE WRECK OF THE
EDMUND FITZGERALD

Off Whitefish Point, Michigan

NOVEMBER 10, 1975

On November 9, 1975, the 729-foot (219m) freighter *Edmund Fitzgerald* loaded with taconite pellets left Superior, Wisconsin, heading east to Detroit via the Sault Ste. Marie locks. That same afternoon, the *Arthur M. Anderson* set out from Two Harbors, Minnesota, also loaded with taconite and heading for the Soo. At 2 a.m. on November 10, 1975, the National Weather Service issued a special storm advisory. Captain Ernest McSorley of the *Fitzgerald* and Captain Bernie Cooper of the *Anderson* discussed the forecast over the radio with some concern. They decided they would continue northeast, staying in the lee of the Canadian shore, rather than heading directly to Whitefish Bay at the east end of Lake Superior.

By that afternoon, as predicted, the waves were 12 to 16 feet (3.6-5m) high and the wind was clocked at 90 mph (144kph). Snow pelted down as the freighters headed almost directly into the mounting seas. Captain Cooper and First Mate Roy Anderson watched the radarscope from the pilothouse of the *Anderson* as the *Fitzgerald*, ahead of them at this point, aimed north of Caribou Island where there was a dangerous shoal. Cooper remarked that the *Fitzgerald* was quite close to it.

Soon after, Morgan Clark relieved Anderson in the pilothouse and the two mates and Cooper stood talking. At 3:30 p.m. conversation in the *Anderson* pilothouse was interrupted by a call from Captain McSorley of the *Fitzgerald*. They had a fence rail down, two vents lost or damaged, and the vessel had developed a list. McSorley was concerned and said he was slowing down so that the *Anderson* could catch up and be on hand should the problems worsen. An hour later, another call from McSorley—the radar wasn't working, and

200 LB. BELL RAISED FROM THE WRECK IN 1995
With permission from victims' families, the ship's bell was raised as a memorial. It is housed at the Great Lakes Shipwreck Museum, Whitefish Point, Michigan.

QUICK DEATH

(Top) The Coast Guard inquiry concluded that the Edmund Fitzgerald had taken on water and sunk because of faulty hatch covers. The freighter went down quickly and the crew had no time to launch the lifeboats or don the life jackets that were recovered (below).

would the *Anderson* provide navigational assistance? For the next several hours the *Anderson* kept track of the *Fitzgerald* as they both pushed on hoping to reach Whitefish Bay that night.

Between 5 and 5:30 p.m. Captain Cedric Woodard of the *Avafors* called the *Fitzgerald* to warn that the Whitefish light radio beacon wasn't working, due to a power failure. Woodard overheard McSorley tell a crewmember not to allow anyone on deck. What was happening on the *Fitzgerald*? McSorley told Woodard that the *Fitzgerald* had a bad list and they were in one of the worst seas he'd ever been in.

Cooper later concurred with this report, saying that the *Anderson* had as much as 12 feet (3.6m) of water on the deck during the same period. At around 6:30 p.m. a massive wave, at least 30 feet (9m) high, had buried the *Anderson's* after cabins and smashed a lifeboat. A second wave, even larger, had washed over the vessel's bridge deck, 35 feet (10.5m) above the waterline. These same two waves, Cooper later hypothesized, would have reached the *Fitzgerald* at about 7:15 p.m.

At 7:10 p.m. Morgan Clark radioed the *Fitzgerald* to warn of a hazard on the radar and inquired about any new problems. The response was "We are holding our own." With the words still hanging in the air, the *Fitzgerald* abruptly disappeared from the *Anderson's* radar screen. Shocked, Clark searched the water for the *Fitzgerald's* silhouette in case there had been a power failure on board. He found nothing. He radioed the freighter *Nanfri*, which was ahead of them, but they couldn't see the *Fitzgerald* either.

Cooper then radioed the U.S. Coast Guard, who tried repeatedly to reach the *Fitzgerald*. No response! By 9:15 p.m. the Coast Guard Air Station at Traverse City, Michigan, had dispatched a helicopter. Two Coast Guard cutters were also headed to the last known position of the *Fitzgerald*. The *Anderson* and two other freighters, the *William Clay Ford* and the *Hilda Marjanne*, left the safety of Whitefish Bay to join the

search that continued through the night. At 8 a.m. on November 11, the *Anderson* finally spotted a lifeboat from the *Fitzgerald*. Close inspection determined that the crew had not launched the lifeboat, but rather it had been torn from the deck when the *Fitzgerald* was sucked down. By the time the search was suspended on November 13, both of the *Fitzgerald*'s 25-person rafts had been found along with life jackets, life rings, a flood light, several lines and other pieces of wreckage, but the hull had vanished. None of the 29 crewmembers' bodies were found.

An 18-month investigation was launched by the U.S. Coast Guard to answer the question of what happened to this "Queen of the Lakes." When the freighter was launched on June 7, 1958, at the Great Lakes Engineering Works at River Rouge, Michigan, it was the largest lake freighter yet built and it quickly became a favorite with ship-watchers and photographers. The ship's captain was a veteran of the lakes, with 44 years of sailing experience.

Despite an exhaustive investigation, the cause of the wreck has never been settled. The Coast Guard concluded that the most probable cause of the sinking was a loss of buoyancy and stability following the flooding of the cargo hold because of inadequate hatch covers. The Lake Carrier's Association and others in the industry disagreed with this conclusion. They argued that, unknown to the crew, the *Fitzgerald* had bottomed on the shoal north of Caribou Island, tearing a hole in the hull. All agreed that water in the hold eventually sunk the vessel. The Coast Guard concluded that "the end was so rapid and catastrophic that there was no time to warn the crew, to attempt to launch lifeboats or life rafts, to don life jackets, or even make a distress call."

VIEWS OF DESTRUCTION

A diorama by Richard Sullivan of the Edmund Fitzgerald *on the lake bottom. It shows the vessel in two pieces, the aft section upside down. (Inset) Two lifeboats were recovered during the search for the missing vessel, but they did not contain any survivors.*

RAFT TO SAFETY

This family boards a raft to escape the flames that ripped through their town, Peshtigo, Wisconsin, in October 1871. An eyewitness described the scene, "large wooden houses torn from their foundations and caught up like straws by two opposing currents of air which raised them till they came in contact with the streams of fire."

LAKE MICHIGAN

FIRE!

The blackened remains of the Phoenix were towed, still smoking, into Sheboygan, Wisconsin. The industrious Jimmie Berry was able to salvage globs of melted gold, which he used to buy two cows—said to provide the first milk in the town.

FIRE ABOARD THE *PHOENIX*

Off Sheboygan, Wisconsin

NOVEMBER 11, 1847

On November 11, 1847, the passenger steamer *Phoenix* set out from Buffalo bound for Milwaukee. The staterooms and steerage cabins were packed with about 270 passengers; most were Dutch immigrants, carrying an estimated $50,000 in gold to purchase lands in the West. The *Phoenix's* bad luck began when Captain Sweet fell and fractured his knee.

Two hours after leaving Manitowoc, Wisconsin, a fireman reported to Second Engineer William Owen that the pumps were not supplying water to the boilers, as they should be. Inexplicably, Owen ignored not only this warning, but also a second one. Just before 4 a.m., smoke was discovered and traced to the boilers, which had overheated and set the nearby woodwork ablaze. Even with the help of some steerage passengers, the crew could not douse the fire.

On deck, three lifeboats were launched, two of them commanded by Captain Sweet and Mate Watts, who fully intended to return for more passengers. But by the time the boats reached shore, about ten miles (16km) north of Sheboygan, the men were nearly frozen and in no condition to return. On board the doomed *Phoenix*, the grim realization that the lifeboats were not returning began to sink in and scores began jumping into the icy water to escape the raging inferno.

Meanwhile, the blaze was spotted in Sheboygan and a rescue boat, the *Delaware*, was dispatched. On arrival two hours after the start of the blaze, the would-be rescuers found only three people clinging to the rudder chains of the charred hull. More than two hundred passengers and crew perished.

WHO WAS TO BLAME?

Responsibility for the tragedy was never fixed but some reported that the crew had too much alcohol at Manitowoc. Others said that everyone was tired out from the battle with the storm and were consequently careless.

BLINDED BY THE STORM

Second Mate George Budge of the schooner Augusta *saw the masthead of the* Lady Elgin *in the distance, barely visible in the driving rain, but he couldn't tell how close the vessel was and he turned his attention to getting some of his sails down before the boat was capsized. By the time the two vessels were within sight of each other, it was too late. The* Augusta's *bow drove into the port side of the* Lady Elgin.

QUEEN OF THE LAKES

The *Lady Elgin* Goes Down Off Winnetka, Illinois

SEPTEMBER 8, 1860

The hot topic in the United States, and particularly Wisconsin, in September 1860 was slavery. Governor Alexander Randall of Wisconsin, a vehement opponent, boldly stated that if the federal government did not abolish slavery he would take Wisconsin out of the Union. He sent representatives out to state militia groups to determine his level of support should he be forced to keep his promise. While most were prepared to support him, Captain Garrett Barry of the Union Guard in Milwaukee refused. Randall revoked Barry's commission and ordered his troops to relinquish their weapons. The angry militia quickly organized an excursion to Chicago on the *Lady Elgin* to raise money for new weapons. Called the "Queen of the Lakes," the *Lady Elgin*, a 252-foot (76m) sidewheel passenger steamer, was one of the largest vessels on the lakes and the height of luxury.

On Thursday evening, September 7, over three hundred members and supporters left Milwaukee for Chicago where they planned to sightsee, then march in a parade before returning on Friday night. An elegant evening of dinner and dancing would be the highlight of the return trip.

Arriving at the Chicago docks for the return trip Friday evening, passengers were disappointed to hear that Captain Jack Wilson had postponed their departure, as the weather was not to his liking. The revelers went ahead with their banquet anyway. To the captain, there seemed to be more passengers on board than the night before—revelers that had followed the party back to the docks.

They continued to urge the captain to get underway and at 11:30 p.m. he relented. By 2 a.m. he was regretting his decision. Gale strength winds pounded the boat and drove heavy rain across the decks. Lightning streaked across the black sky. Captain Wilson struggled with the limited visibility while below decks, the party went on.

Unknown to Wilson, the lumber schooner *Augusta* was sailing toward the *Lady Elgin* with a full load of Muskegon pine. The *Augusta's* second mate, George Budge, had seen the *Lady Elgin* in the distance but his immediate concern

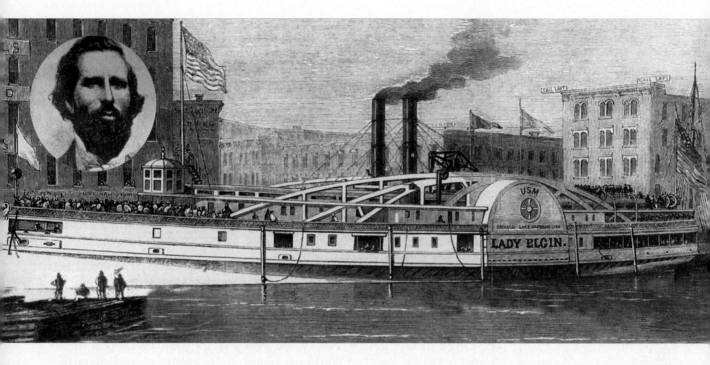

LADY ELGIN AT BERTH

The Lady Elgin *in Chicago River, between Clark and La Salle Streets on September 7, 1860, the day before the disaster. (Inset) Captain Wilson put off departure from Chicago because the weather did not look good but he relented to pressure by passengers and the* Lady Elgin *left the dock at 11:30 p.m.*

was to get some of the sails down before the boat was de-masted. In turn, the *Lady Elgin's* second mate caught a glimpse of the *Augusta's* masthead in a flash of lightning, but could not gauge its direction or proximity because it was carrying no running lights. He alerted Captain Wilson, who judged they were clear of the other vessel, but thought it wise to come over to starboard a few degrees to make sure.

Soon after, the *Augusta's* Captain Malott made his way on deck. Glancing up, he saw the lights of the *Lady Elgin*, just visible in the rain, and yelled to the wheelsman to push the wheel hard to starboard. It was too late. The *Augusta* drove into the side of the *Lady Elgin*.

The *Augusta* recoiled from the impact but its forward rigging caught in the broken timbers of the larger vessel and it was forced to run beside the *Lady Elgin* until the headsail and stay ripped apart, separating the two boats. The crew of the *Augusta* reasonably assumed that their smaller vessel had taken the brunt of the collision and watched in anger as the *Lady Elgin* steamed away. Shouldn't they have asked if the *Augusta* needed assistance?

Their anger was short-lived, however. When the cook went forward to assess the damage, much to everyone's surprise he reported back that there was only a small amount of water leaking in—nothing to cause alarm. Relieved, they made a few repairs and were soon underway. As they worked, Captain Malott periodically looked towards the *Lady Elgin*. Suddenly the steamer made a hard turn to the left. It was heading straight for shore!

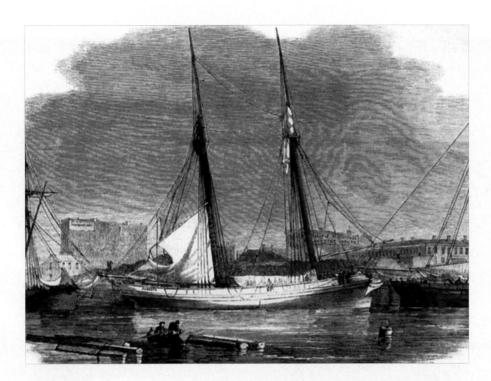

On board the *Lady Elgin*, water was pouring into the lower decks through a gaping hole made by the pointed bow of the *Augusta*. After a quick assessment of the damage, Captain Wilson ordered the wheelsman to steer for shore, nine miles (14.4km) away. The mate rang the ship's bell and blew the steam whistle to alert the passengers and any other nearby vessels. The crew frantically tossed cargo overboard to lighten the load, and in an effort to stem the flow of water rushing in the side, the captain ordered First Mate George Davis to launch one of the four lifeboats to see if they could stuff mattresses and canvas into the wound. Waves immediately swamped the lifeboat and the men had to bail furiously as the *Lady Elgin* moved away from them. A second lifeboat was launched. When a few of the passengers saw more crewmembers being lowered, they assumed they were abandoning ship, and so they jumped into the boat as well, determined not to be left behind. Once the boat was in the water they discovered that there were no oars.

The remaining two lifeboats were never launched. No one knows why. In any case, they would have been totally inadequate since they could only hold a total of 32 people and the steamer was filled with as many as four hundred passengers. Without further warning, the *Lady Elgin* plunged to the bottom of the lake.

Anyone not trapped inside the diving vessel was tossed into the water amongst the floating debris: crates, chairs, barrels and the entire hurricane deck, which had come apart from the hull. Some managed to climb aboard and began

Collision!

The Lady Elgin *and the* Augusta *collide on Lake Michigan during a storm. The wreckage of the* Lady Elgin *was found by salvager Harry Zych in 1989 several miles off Highwood, Illinois. There are four main wreckage fields, which lie in 55 to 60 feet (16.5-18m) of water.*

helping others. Repeatedly pounded by the waves, the deck broke into smaller pieces until only about forty people, including the captain, were left clinging to the largest section. During the night the captain was tireless in his encouragement of the survivors, buoying them up as their resolve faltered. At one point he dove into the water to help a woman who had drifted away from the group and he never returned. He was presumed drowned.

Among the first to reach the shore near Evanston, Illinois, were First Mate Davis and the crew of the first lifeboat. They had managed to bail it out and had rowed after the *Lady Elgin* watching with horror as the boat went down. Nearing the beach they were faced with another obstacle. They would first have to navigate through a violent surf, then scale towering cliffs forty feet (12m) high in order to reach safety. Somehow they did manage to land and scale the cliff in search of help. Soon local residents appeared atop the cliff with blankets, dry clothes and ropes, but they were unsure how to help the passengers who began to drift into shore on makeshift rafts. Some died in the surf only one hundred feet

THE ELEGANT STEAMER
The 252-foot (76m) side-wheeler Lady Elgin, *launched at Buffalo in 1851, was named after the wife of the Governor General of Canada, Lord Elgin.*

(30m) from safety, thrown against the rocks, but many others managed to cling to the rock cliff until they could be helped up over the top.

One brave determined onlooker, Edward Spencer, tied a rope around his waist and was lowered into the breaking waves an amazing sixteen times. After fifteen rescues he collapsed in exhaustion, but managed to build a fire to warm himself. When he saw a man drifting towards the shore, dragging another person, he decided to make one last effort. Over the side he went and managed to save a husband and wife. Today at Northwestern University there is a bronze memorial to his inspirational efforts. Estimates place the number of survivors between 98 and 155.

In the meantime, the *Augusta* had arrived in Chicago without further mishap. Captain Malott and his crew were immediately brought to testify before a quickly assembled Cook County Coroner's jury. A verdict was released the next day, placing blame for the disaster on both vessels. The *Lady Elgin's* officers and owners were criticized for overloading the ship and having too few lifeboats, while the *Augusta's* second mate was reprimanded for not informing his captain immediately upon seeing the lights of the approaching *Lady Elgin.* However, the most severe criticism was directed against the existing navigational laws. By the 1830s both England and France had enacted formal Right of Way rules. Proposals for similar laws in the U.S. had been met with opposition from ship owners and masters, who preferred the existing, rather slack, approach. In 1864 the carnage from accidents such as the sinking of the *Lady Elgin* finally forced Congress to enact the first U.S. navigational law.

FLAMING FIELDS
Families wrapped in wet blankets seek refuge from the flames. Some survived, but others were suffocated as the massive fire consumed all of the available oxygen.

THE PESHTIGO FIRE

Oconto, Brown, Kewaunee, Marinette and Door Counties, Wisconsin, and Menominee County, Michigan

OCTOBER 8, 1871

As churchgoers made their way home after evening service on Sunday, October 8, 1871, they commented on the stagnant air that lay over the small village of Peshtigo, Wisconsin. It had been an exceptionally dry summer and for the past three weeks wildfires had been burning sporadically in areas around the village. The air was heavy with smoke.

Sometime after 8:30 that evening, light, refreshing gusts of wind scuttled dried leaves and dust across the village. Soon after, a faint light appeared on the horizon. This scene quickly changed to a brilliant amber glow punctuated by the roar of an approaching fire.

A tornado-like wind hit Peshtigo, blowing roofs from houses and businesses, followed by the full fury of the fire itself. As sheets of flame leapt over the village, scores of people and animals ran to the Peshtigo River, dodging the flying debris exploding out of the village. Suddenly the bridge gave way and fell into the river, crushing anyone trapped below. In less than an hour the village was annihilated. The survivors had the devastating task of identifying, burying and mourning their lost families and friends while trying to pick up the pieces of their lives in a village that was literally burned off the map.

On October 11, an issue of the *Marinette and Peshtigo Eagle Extra* carried the story of what has been called the worst natural fire in the history of the United States:

> Standing amid the charred and blackened embers, with the frightfully mutilated corpses of men, women, children, horses, shed, barn, out-house or structure of any kind swept from the earth as with the very besom of destruction, our emotions cannot be described in language.

In the six affected counties, approximately twelve hundred deaths were attributed to the fire, but with about eight hundred dead, Peshtigo had been the hardest hit.

CITY IN FLAMES

Chicago residents flee over the Randolph Street Bridge, one of two major bridges (the other was the Lake Street Bridge) used to escape the West Division. Many were trampled and crushed in mass panic.

THE GREAT CHICAGO FIRE

Chicago, Illinois

OCTOBER 8, 1871

For many historians, the Great Chicago Fire of 1871 was a disaster waiting to happen. Chicago, the "Queen of the West," grew from a population of 4000 in 1840 to more than 334,000 in 1870, and 90 percent of its buildings were made entirely of wood. The summer of 1871 was the driest in the city's history and the *Tribune* staff, sitting smugly in their new "fireproof" building, ran an editorial warning that behind their marble fronts, Chicago's buildings were tinder waiting to be ignited. In fact, fire was a common problem in Chicago. Between 1858 and 1871, the city was plagued by nearly 3700 of them. In 1868 a fire on Lake Street had caused more than $2 million in losses and started a mass migration to the new business district developing along State Street. The high number of fires even spurred Lloyd's of London to stop insuring property in Chicago.

The city was also the center of the American woodworking industry with furniture mills, lumber yards, and paint and varnish shops dotting the landscape. As well, with seventeen grain elevators, it boasted the largest grain market in the world. However, because of Chicago's new waterworks, opened in 1867 on the north side, warnings such as the *Tribune's* were generally ignored. The water tower, nearly one hundred feet (30m) high, symbolized a new confidence in the city and its ability to stave off fires.

In 1871 only 1.5 inches (4cm) of rain fell between the 4th of July and October. Firefighters battled as many as twenty fires a day in the week leading up to the disaster—far more than the previous year's average of two fires a day. The crews were undermanned and exhausted.

A FIRE WAITING TO HAPPEN

Many considered Chicago ripe for a fatal conflagration. Ninety percent of the city's buildings were wood and between 1858 and 1871 the city was plagued by nearly 3700 fires.

THE NOTORIOUS COW

Did Mrs. O'Leary's cow start the Great Chicago Fire? While the fire began in the vicinity of the family's barn and some claim to have found pieces of a lantern that the cow is said to have knocked over, most historians agree that the story was dreamed up by a police reporter named Michael Ahern. On the 40th anniversary of the fire he admitted that he and two colleagues invented the story. (Inset) Drawing claiming to be of the actual O'Leary lamp.

The source of the Great Chicago Fire is still shrouded in controversy. The most famous legend is that of the cranky O'Leary cow, who is said to have kicked over a lantern in the O'Leary barn at Jefferson and DeKoven Streets. This story is now generally accepted as the fabrication of a newspaper reporter. Other accounts place blame on partygoers who may have been sneaking into the barn for fresh cream. Most accounts do agree, however, that the fire started in the vicinity of the O'Leary barn.

A 9:15 p.m. on October 8, 1871, the watch at the Little Giant Fire Company spotted fire leaping skyward. The fire crew dragged themselves from their bunks and arrived on DeKoven Street to find three barns (including the O'Leary barn), a paint shop, and a shed engulfed in flames.

The inferno had already been burning for nearly an hour. Because of a mix-up, no other fire company had responded. The blaze rapidly became too much for the firefighters to handle and flames spread northward. Burning embers flew through the air and landed on the steeple of St. Paul's Roman Catholic Church, four blocks away. After engulfing this building, the blaze moved on to a factory and Bateman's lumber mill, stacked with furniture, lumber and wooden shingles.

By 1:30 a.m. the city's gas works were threatened but thanks to a quick-thinking city engineer, most of the gas had been emptied from the tanks. Another half-hour saw the courthouse burn. Prisoners in the basement cells were released with the exception of five murderers, who were taken down to the river in handcuffs. Flames jumped easily back and forth over the Chicago River, putting to rest the idea that the river would act as a firebreak.

The streets were overrun with people fleeing the flames. They saved whatever they could drag, some pushing wheelbarrows full of personal items, others carrying blankets and mattresses. Wagons and coaches were hired at exorbitant prices to carry goods out of reach of the fire. By 3:30 a.m. the waterworks succumbed, ending the city's pumping capacity. Some people sought refuge in Lake Michigan,

while others found sanctuary in the city cemetery until flames scorched that as well.

In the business district, the new Grand Pacific and Bigelow hotels burned before they could host a single guest. The Tremont House burned for the fourth time in its history. Its industrious manager, John B. Drake, managed to salvage the money from the hotel's safe and stashed it in a pillowcase along with a few pieces of the hotel's silver. As he ran through the crowded streets towards his home he saw the Michigan Avenue Hotel, which was still unscathed. With his pillowcase of money, he offered to buy, on the spot, the hotel's lease and its furnishings. The manager looked at Drake in disbelief, but agreed to the deal, fully believing the hotel would never survive. A hasty contract was drawn up and Drake paid an advance of $1000 dollars in cash.

By this time hundreds were fleeing from the roaring flames. The sky was aglow and a storm of hot cinders rained down on the streets. Some unscrupulous citizens saw the panic as an opportunity to loot empty stores and bars. A few accounts describe drunken gangs of people rampaging through the streets, adding

WITHIN THE THRONG OF PEOPLE
Many panicked residents dragged possessions such as straw mattresses and furniture through the streets. These flammable items added to the nightmare when they ignited into flames from the rain of cinders that showered the crowd.

First National Bank and its Ruins
(Above) Many banks were destroyed when the hurricane of flames leveled the business district. Jets of fire even consumed so-called "fireproof" safes.

Cooling off a Safe
(Right) What safes couldn't protect the bank staff took care of. A cashier at 2nd National paid an expressman $1000 to carry a box through the fire to the railway depot. It was later found at a Milwaukee bank holding treasure valued at $600,000.

to the mass confusion. In at least one case, firefighters had to turn their hoses on the unruly crowd.

Factories along the river lay in ruins and the bridges over the river's south branch were destroyed. On the north side the fire reached LaSalle Street, then backtracked, burning anything left untouched by the first wave. Those taking refuge at the water's edge were forced into the water as the heat intensified.

By 11 a.m. the last row of houses on the south side, Terrace Row, was destroyed and by afternoon the business section began to burn out. Only the fire to the north continued its march. By nightfall all of the larger fires had slowed; dying embers lit the blackened landscape. The last house to burn was on Fullerton Avenue, 25 hours after the fire had started. A few minutes before midnight rain began to fall. The final reckoning? Three and a half square miles (9km^2) in the central part of the city destroyed, 15,700 buildings gone, 100,000 made homeless. Nearly three hundred were known dead and possibly countless others were never reported. How would Chicago ever recover from such a blow?

In fact, the city wasted no time in picking up the pieces. The next day, five thousand special police were appointed to patrol the area to stop any looting. The Mayor prohibited the sale of whiskey and fixed the price of bread. Clothing and food poured in from all over the United States and tents provided shelter for the homeless. Basic services sprang up around the city in makeshift sheds.

On the negative side, many lives were irrevocably changed. Rents skyrocketed because of the housing shortage, and new restrictions on flammable building materials made construction expensive. Tensions increased between the classes, especially when

PILES OF CLOTHING FOR THE HOMELESS

(Left) Trains from all over the United States delivered donations of money, food, clothing and supplies. One of the biggest jobs of the relief effort went to the Lost and Found Committee who reunited entire families that had been separated by the turmoil.

THE HORROR

(Lower) For many, the fire was only one part of the trauma. The other part came in seeing so many dead. There were pitiful sights, such as a charred woman and child near the Sands Brewery. The mother had buried her baby in the sand and placed herself over the hole to give protection.

American-born reformers convinced Mayor Medill to enforce an existing ban on Sunday drinking. Irish and German immigrants took this as a direct attack on the salons and beer halls in which they gathered, which it certainly was. Politics became increasingly class-driven and eventually Medill resigned his office and left Chicago.

In many ways, however, the fire was responsible for much of what we see in Chicago today. As a result of the recovery effort, known as the "Great Rebuilding," residential neighborhoods became more distinguishable from the business district, the downtown core expanded and distinctive skyscrapers replaced the old wooden structures.

MICHIGAN TIMBER

(Above) Michigan was the nation's leading lumber producer between 1869 and 1900. Poor lumber practices led to the devastating fires of 1871 and 1881. (Right) Cover of The Flaming Forest, *published by the Tuscola County Advertiser after the fire of 1881. "Gruesome, horrible and awesome though it is…The Great Fire of 1881 is a part of the Thumb's heritage…and through it we more fully appreciate the agony and the suffering by which this great area was tamed and brought into flower."*

MICHIGAN TIMBER FIRES

Oconto, Brown, Kewaunee, Marinette and Door Counties, Wisconsin, and Menominee County, Michigan

OCTOBER 1871 AND SEPTEMBER 1881

October 1871 was a devastating month for fires in Michigan, Wisconsin, and Illinois. The story of the Great Chicago Fire and the Peshtigo Fire are well documented but there was a third conflagration that occurred in the Michigan's northern Thumb area. What conditions could cause such massive destruction?

In his *History of the Great Fires in Chicago and the West*, written in 1871, the Rev. E.J. Goodspeed states:

> In our foolish American haste we have wastefully cut down the trees, dried up the springs, raised the temperature so that precipitation of moisture is reduced, and have driven the rain away in useless clouds of invisible vapor over the Atlantic. We have prayed for rain one day of the week and driven it away with an axe on six. Now, whose fault was it?

The summer of 1871 had been extremely dry and fires broke out throughout Michigan State, fueled by debris from the logging industry. On the night of October 8, 1871, hot winds in the Saginaw Valley and Thumb region turned the flames of several land clearing fires into one massive inferno that wiped out the cities of Holland and Manistee and spread as far as Port Huron on Lake Huron. Approximately two hundred deaths would result.

Ten years later, a larger fire known as the Thumb Fire would sweep the same area, taking 282 lives, blackening a million acres, and destroying Tuscola, Huron, Sanilac and St. Clair Counties. Conditions were similar to those in 1871—a severe summer drought and uncontrolled land-clearing fires. The resulting holocaust was intensified by the piles of deadwood and debris left over from the 1871 fire.

Fires had always been part of normal life in the forests of Michigan, but wasteful cutting practices were credited with the huge increase in the number and intensity of forest fires. It was not until the early 1900s that Michigan citizens began to worry about the future of their forests and introduced the era of conservation.

CHICORA VANISHES

The Chicora *disappeared on January 21, 1895. According to one report, the ship's dog was found wandering on the beach near St. Joseph a few days after the accident.*

BAD OMEN

Chicora lost between Milwaukee, Wisconsin, and St. Joseph, Michigan

JANUARY 21, 1895

Mr. John H. Graham, President of Graham Morton Transportation Company, surveyed the barometer in his St. Joseph home at 4 a.m. the morning of January 21, 1895. It registered 28, the lowest he had ever seen, and two of his ships were scheduled to sail within hours. He raced down to the dock in time to stop the *Petoskey* from casting off and ordered the telegraph operator to send a message to the second ship, the 217-foot (65m) passenger and package steamer *Chicora* in Milwaukee. The telegram was sent through to Milwaukee and a bike courier was dispatched. He arrived just as the *Chicora* pulled away from the dock but no one could hear his shouts above the noise of the boilers and churning propeller.

Soon after departure, the *Chicora* ran into appalling conditions as a ferocious winter storm swept across Lake Michigan. When the vessel did not arrive in St. Joseph on time, the alarm was sounded and Mr. Graham sent telegrams to ports along the route, hoping the *Chicora* had taken refuge from the storm. The answers were all the same: "No, the *Chicora* wasn't here." His worst fears were confirmed when wreckage began to wash ashore. No one had survived.

Was there more to the disaster than atrocious weather? A superstitious dread had risen among the crew and Captain Edward Stines after a passenger, during the trip to Milwaukee, had shot a duck that landed on the deck in the middle of the lake. While the boat was loading in Milwaukee, they repeatedly referred to the shooting as an evil omen.

In May 2001, members of the Southwest Michigan Underwater Preserve located what they believe to be the steamer *Chicora* in about 300 feet (90m) of water off Saugatuck, Michigan, but their discovery has yet to be confirmed.

EXTRA | The Chicago Daily Tribune. | EXTRA

VOLUME LXII.—NO. 818.   THURSDAY, DECEMBER 31, 1903—SIXTEEN PAGES.   ☆ PRICE TWO CE.

FIRE IN THE IROQUOIS THEATER KILLS 571 AND INJURES 350 PERSON

"ABSOLUTELY FIREPROOF"

The Iroquois Theater, billed as "absolutely fireproof," was brand new when it caught fire on December 30, 1903, with 1900 patrons inside. (Top inset) Officials survey the damage to the balcony. (Bottom inset) A mother searches for her children.

IROQUOIS THEATER FIRE

Chicago, Illinois

DECEMBER 30, 1903

The newly built Iroquois Theater was packed with nearly 1900 patrons on December 30, 1903, for the popular musical Mr. Blue Bird. Only a month old, the spectacular theater with its mahogany and marble was billed as "absolutely fireproof," the "safest" building of its kind in Chicago.

During the second act, sparks from an overloaded electrical circuit ignited a drapery behind the stage. Stagehand William McMullen, who was stationed on a catwalk, tried to snuff out the tiny flickers, but they were two inches (5cm) beyond his reach. Quickly, the flames spread to the adjoining scenery. The on-duty fireman, with only two tubes of firefighting substance called Kilfyres at his disposal, failed to stop the fire. The star comedian, Eddie Foy, shouted to lower the asbestos curtain to keep the fire from spreading into the audience but the curtain snagged halfway down and so when fleeing patrons threw open the exit doors, the curtain acted as a flue. Fueled by the fresh air, a fireball shot out from under the curtain and reached the patrons in the first balcony, burning them in their seats.

The explosion that followed lifted the entire roof. The hysterical crowd on the upper floors pushed and trampled each other in their race to the stairwells and fire exits, which turned out to have no ladders. In the crush, patrons were pushed off the tiny balconies and fell to their death. In less than thirty minutes the fire was out, but the gruesome discovery of bodies piled ten feet high around windows and in stairwells awaited the rescue workers. Six hundred and one people died in the fire.

An investigation began immediately. A coroner's jury found fault both with the theater and with city officials although no one was criminally charged. The jury pointed out that the theater had inadequate exits (some were locked to prevent people from sneaking in), totally inadequate fire-fighting equipment and untrained staff.

FLEEING THE INFERNO

A survivor described the scene: "The screams of the children for their mothers and mothers for their children I shall carry in my memory to my dying day."

PULLED FROM THE OVERTURNED *EASTLAND*

On some areas of the overturned Eastland rescuers cut into the hull with torches. One man who had begun to use a torch on the boat was rudely shoved aside by Captain Pedersen and ordered to stop. He refused. "After we got rid of Pedersen," he told newsmen, "we took 40 people, all alive, out of that hole."

CAPSIZING OF THE *EASTLAND*

Chicago, Illinois

JULY 24, 1915

For weeks, employees at the Western Electric Company of Chicago had been buzzing about the Hawthorne Club picnic and excursion to Michigan City, Indiana. The trip was an annual event for the nine thousand employees, and for several weeks the Hawthorne Club newspaper, the *Jubilator*, had been asking, "Are you all ready for the big event? Get your tickets early...children under five free!" There would be tug o'wars, sack races, baseball games, and a large parade with floats, including one with a scene showing the linking of New York to San Francisco by telephone line (the company had manufactured the equipment for the line).

Six boats had been hired: the *Theodore Roosevelt*, the *Petoskey*, the *Racine*, the *Rochester*, the *Maywood* and the *Eastland*. By 6:30 a.m. on Saturday, July 24, 1915, five thousand picnickers had already arrived at the docks.

The crew of the 275-foot (83m) *Eastland* had only managed a few hours of sleep as they had been busy cleaning the boat after a moonlight cruise, but shortly before 7 a.m. the boat was ready. Luman A. Lebdell and Hurdus G. Oakley manned the single gangplank, counting the passengers as they embarked. (The *Eastland* was certified for 2570 people.) As more people hurried on board, the vessel began to list to starboard, which was closest to the dock (a normal occurrence during boarding). Chief Engineer Joseph M. Erickson ordered the port ballast tanks filled until the vessel could right itself, but soon after the *Eastland* began to list to port and so the starboard tanks were partially filled. By the time the *Eastland* had reached capacity, the list had increased to 15 degrees. For a few short minutes, the vessel leveled off, only to tilt again. All the while, Erickson was ordering the ship's ballast tanks to be alternately filled and emptied in an effort to stabilize the vessel.

DISASTER WAITING TO HAPPEN
Before the capsizing of the Eastland *on July 24, 1915, there were two near-miss incidents where the top-heavy steamer had almost capsized.*

SAFE ABOVE THE WATERLINE

Hundreds of picnickers managed to climb onto the side of the Eastland *when it rolled over. Some didn't even get their feet wet!*

On the Clark Street bridge Mike Javanco, returning from market with a wagon full of vegetables, spotted the listing *Eastland* and shouted to the passengers, "Get off, the boat's turning over!" The crowd just laughed. On the dock, Harbormaster Adam F. Weckler also saw the list and yelled up to the captain, "Are you ready captain?"

By 7:23 a.m. the list had worsened and passengers were directed to move to starboard away from their port side view of the river. The *Eastland* stubbornly continued to lean—25 degrees, then 30, then 45, as chairs, picnic baskets, and other items slid all over the decks. The crew realized the danger and many reportedly leaped from the *Eastland* to the dock. From the starboard bridge Captain Pedersen yelled, "Open the inside doors and let the people off!" The passengers began to panic. Many pulled themselves up to the starboard side and made their way down gangways or any other possible exit but for most passengers it was too late. At 7:30 a.m. the *Eastland* rolled on its side, spilling hundreds of screaming picnickers into the water and trapping hundreds more below deck. A few hundred passengers had managed to climb over the starboard rail and were safe on the exposed underside of the *Eastland*.

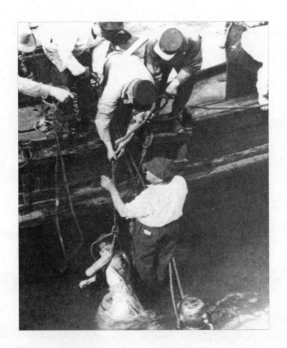

CASUALTIES
(Left) A victim is lifted from the ship's hull. Because travelers were part of a company picnic, many women and children were casualties of the disaster. (Right) Worker recovers the body of a child.

One eyewitness described the scene:

I shall never be able to forget what I saw. People were struggling in the water, clustered so thickly that they literally covered the surface of the river. A few were swimming; the rest were floundering about, some clinging to a life raft that had floated free, others clutching at anything they could reach—bits of wood, at each other, grabbing each other, pulling each other down, and screaming! The screaming was the most horrible of all.

Those on shore sprang into action and threw pieces of wood and crates—anything that would float—into the river. Firefighters, the Coast Guard, police officers and nearby boats pitched in to haul people out of the water.

Those trapped inside the *Eastland's* hull could be heard pounding against the hull in desperation. Rescuers used blowtorches to cut holes for the terrified passengers. Forty escaped from one such hole.

Soon the rescuers had to turn to the grisly business of recovering bodies. Numbered tags were attached to each body with information such as gender, approximate age and a description of their clothing. The nearby Second Regiment Armory was turned into a temporary morgue and by 11 p.m. the crowd of inquisitive spectators had grown so large that it blocked the entrance to the armory. A frustrated Coroner Hoffman climbed a stepladder and shouted, "In the name of God, I ask you to go away and let those seeking relatives and friends come in and identify their dead." Five hundred and twenty-six bodies were recovered that night. The toll eventually reached 844 (some reports say 835).

844 DEAD

Bodies are lined up at the nearby Second Regiment Armory for identification. One child, No. 396, lay unclaimed for eight days.

The Chicago media was struck by the story of No. 396, a small unidentified boy who lay in the morgue, unclaimed. "Who is the little feller?" they asked. Not until eight days after the accident was the boy finally identified as Willie Novotny. Willie's grandmother had been in a state of shock at the deaths of her daughter, son-in-law and eight-year-old granddaughter Mamie and had failed to notify the authorities that there was still one Novotny missing—Willie.

The public outcry over the capsizing was quick and furious. Captain Pedersen the first mate were placed under arrest at the scene and on their way to City Hall an angry mob assaulted them, despite a police escort of twenty men. Separate investigations by city, state and federal authorities began almost immediately.

They found that the *Eastland* was well known in the industry for having a recurring problem with listing. John Devereaux York, a naval architect from

Chicago, had warned authorities in a letter two years earlier, "You are aware of the condition of the S.S. *Eastland* and unless structural defects are remedied to prevent listing...there may be a serious accident."

There was also the question of the boat's certification. On July 2, 1915, the *Eastland* had been issued a temporary certificate for 2570 people, an increase from the 2253 passengers it was certified to carry on June 15 of the same year.

STEAMER ON ITS SIDE

Another view of the Eastland *on its side in* Chicago Harbor.

Robert Reid, the Federal Inspector of Hulls for Grand Haven, explained that the certificate had been issued after a call from William H. Hull, the vice-president of the Indiana Transportation Company, owners of the *Eastland*. Reid came under intense scrutiny by the newspapers, which accused him of issuing the certificate because of his close friendships with some employees in the Indiana Transportation Company. After all, they pointed out, Reid's son-in-law was Joseph M. Erickson, the chief engineer on the *Eastland*.

The Hawthorne Club and the Western Electric Company were also criticized, although they could not have foreseen the disaster. They were accused of a "hard sell" campaign to sell tickets for the excursion. Anthony Thies, who lost two daughters, said, "I begged them to stay home but Anna told me she would lose her job if she didn't go. She said the foreman of her department had warned her that unless she and Agnes went, their names would be scratched from the payroll." Other grieving family, friends and survivors told similar stories.

Meanwhile, the various inquests argued over who had jurisdiction in the accident. At the time, maritime law only allowed for damages to be claimed up to the value of the hull. The *Eastland* was sold for $46,000 at auction in December. This sum would be divided among nearly one thousand claimants when the final decision was handed down by the United States Circuit Court of Appeals in August 1935, twenty years after the accident. They concluded that the company "was liable only to the extent of the salvage of the vessel; that the boat was seaworthy; that the operators had taken proper precautions and that the responsibility was traced to an engineer who neglected to fill the ballast tanks properly."

SAILORS IN TROUBLE
The Navadoc *broke up off Ludington, Michigan. The heroic efforts of the crew of the fishing tug* Three Brothers *saved 17 of 19 men on board.*

RESCUED
Near Ludington, Michigan, crew are taken off the beached car ferry City of Flint 32 *with a breeches buoy.*

NOVEMBER WITCHES

Armistice Day Storm, Great Lakes

NOVEMBER 11, 1940

On Armistice Day, November 11, 1940, the Midwest region of the United States was hit by a terrifying storm, reminiscent of the historic gales of 1913 that had wreaked havoc on the Great Lakes. On shore, raging winds toppled church steeples, telephone lines and rooftops and brought driving snow to Wisconsin, South Dakota, Nebraska, Minnesota, Iowa and Michigan. Further south, it stranded hundreds of duck hunters along the shores of the Mississippi River and was blamed for 144 deaths.

On the water, Lake Michigan bore the brunt with winds reaching as high as 125 mph (200kph). All over the lake, vessels were in trouble. On the east shore at Ludington, the car ferry *City of Flint 32* was blown ashore, while a nearby fish tug *Three Brothers* managed to save seventeen men aboard the doomed *Navadoc*. The freighter *Frank J. Peterson* was beached at Hog Island, while another freighter, the *Navadoc*, went aground off Naubinway at the northern tip of the lake.

Among the worst disasters were the complete loss of both the 380-foot (114m) steamship *Anna C. Minch* and the 420-foot (126m) steel freighter *William B. Davock*. All hands perished—24 on the *Minch* and 32 on the *Davock*. The *Minch* was found a mile and a half (2.4km) south of the pier at Pentwater with her mast still above water. Bodies from both ships washed up along the shore near Pentwater and Ludington, leading some to speculate that they had collided.

In all, 59 sailors, mainly on Lake Michigan, were lost. Because November had always been a dangerous month for shipping on the Great Lakes, the storms were given the nickname "Witches of November."

BURIED ON EXCELSIOR BLVD.

Up to 26 inches (65cm) of snow fell in Minneapolis and 80 mph (128kph) winds caused 20-foot (6m) snowdrifts during the Armistice Day Storm.

DID IT BREAK IN TWO?

The 640-foot (192m) steel bulk carrier Carl D. Bradley *lies south of Gull Island in 365 feet (110m) of water. Sonar equipment shows the wreck to be in one piece but crewmen Mays and Fleming have always contended that they saw the vessel break in two.*

"Pretty Ripe For Too Much Weather"

Sinking of the *Carl D. Bradley*, Gull Island, Michigan

November 18, 1958

It was to be the last trip of the season for the 640-foot (192m) steel bulk carrier *Carl D. Bradley* when it left Buffington, Indiana, bound for Rogers City late on November 17, 1958. Captain Roland Bryan and his crew were eager to be heading home. Although the weather was not ideal, no one wanted to delay the boat's departure.

Over the course of the season there had been some concern about the *Bradley's* condition. In a letter to his girlfriend, Captain Bryan had written, "This boat is getting pretty ripe for too much weather." The aging boat was scheduled to have major repairs and a new $800,000 cargo hold installed over the winter.

By the next afternoon the weather had worsened steadily until the wind was blowing between 60 and 65 mph (97-105kph) and Lake Michigan was spewing up 25-foot (7.5m) waves. At 5:30 p.m. the *Bradley* had passed Cana Island and was turning to head across the open lake when deckhands Frank Mays and Gary Price heard a loud thud unlike any of the regular noises made by the rusting hull. They hurried up to the main deck and found a wide crack running through the middle of the deck and saw the stern beginning to drop. The ship was breaking apart.

Within a mere fifteen minutes, the *Bradley* broke in two and sank bow first. There was barely enough time to send a mayday. Trying to reach a life raft on the deck behind the pilothouse, two crewmen, Fleming and Mays were thrown overboard when the boat lurched to port. They came upon a raft that had been swept off the deck, climbed up, then pulled deckhands Gary Strzelecki and Dennis Meredith to safety. The four men struggled to keep the raft upright, but lost Meredith when it flipped over. During the night their precarious craft flipped several times and eventually the struggle to survive proved too much for Strzelecki—he floated away, despite the urging of Mays and Fleming. The only survivors were Mays and Fleming, who were picked up by a Coast Guard cutter 14 hours after the boat went down. In all, Rogers City would lose 33 citizens in yet another November tragedy.

*'The engine came off
and fluttered to the ground'*

*There were just pieces
of bodies, nothing alive'*

*'It looked like an
atomic bomb explosion'*

272 killed in Chicago plane disaster

FIELD OF DEBRIS

*(Top) Newspaper quotes eye witnesses. (Above) The numbered flags indicate the
number of bodies buried at each placement in the rubble. (Inset right) An ama-
teur photographer captured this picture of Flight 191 moments before it crashed.*

FLIGHT 191

DC-10 Crashes After Takeoff From
O'Hare International, Chicago, Illinois

MAY 25, 1979

Memorial Day weekend 1979 marks one of the worst air disasters in the United States. American Airlines flight 191 left Chicago's O'Hare International Airport bound for Los Angeles with a full complement of passengers. Seconds after the wide-body jet lifted off the runway, one of its three engines crashed to the tarmac. About 30 seconds later, at a height of 400 feet (120m), the left wing dipped and the plane plunged straight into the ground. All 271 passengers and crew plus two people on the ground were killed.

One witness likened the scene to an atomic explosion and a Chicago newspaper reported that the smoke and flames reached twice as high as had the jet itself. The rubble was studded with stakes bearing colored streamers—red indicating one body; yellow, two or three bodies; black, five bodies. A temporary morgue had to be set up in an American Airlines hangar.

What could possibly have caused such an immediate and devastating crash? A United Airlines pilot was quick to come to the defense of the pilot, saying, "in most cases recovery by the pilot is almost hopeless, particularly at take-off." The official investigation laid most of the blame on the American Airlines mechanics who had not followed the proper procedure when removing the engine for maintenance in March of that year. Investigators had found a three-inch (7.5cm) bolt on the runway that had broken in two and most likely caused the engine to drop off. The Federal Aviation Association was also criticized for failing to monitor the airline's maintenance practices.

LAKE
HURON

E. Tucker

SEARCH FOR SUNKEN TREASURE

The Pewabic *went down with a load of valuable copper; five divers lost their lives attempting to recover it. In all, 55 tons of copper was recovered.*

SISTER SHIPS *PEWABIC* AND *METEOR* COLLIDE

Near Alpena, Michigan

AUGUST 9, 1865

The first mate of the *Pewabic*, George Cleveland, had spotted the lights of their sister ship, the *Meteor*, when it was well off the port bow and instructed the wheelsman to steer to starboard in preparation for a port-to-port passing. Around the same time, the engineer on watch in the engine room glanced out the door on the port side and quickly called Captain George McKay. Instead of seeing the red running light of the *Meteor*, which would indicate the port side, McKay could clearly see a green light. The ships were on a collision course! Reaching the hurricane deck, McKay ordered the starboard engine stopped and the wheel turned hard to starboard. Too late. The *Meteor* slammed into the side of the *Pewabic*, which sank in less than five minutes.

Some passengers managed to climb over to the *Meteor*, while others were rescued from the water by *Meteor* lifeboats. Captain McKay crossed over just before his ship, the *Pewabic*, sank. Reports state that no sooner had he arrived on the *Meteor*'s deck than he accused Captain Wilson, who was directing the rescue efforts, of wanting to drown them all "in order that there might be no one to testify at an investigation."

In fact, an inquiry by the Board of Steamship Inspectors found that it was McKay's last-minute maneuvering to starboard that had caused the collision. A public outcry over the estimated 125 deaths contributed to the conviction of First Mate Cleveland, who was found guilty of manslaughter and sentenced to prison for his role in the collision. McKay had his license revoked. Both decisions were overturned on appeal and both men went on to distinguished careers as merchant marine officers.

HOLED BY SISTER SHIP

Marine artist Robert McGreevy's painting of the Pewabic *before the fateful collision.*

SHOULD A CAPTAIN GO DOWN WITH HIS SHIP?
Captain John Savage died in controversy when he chose to occupy one of the Asia's few lifeboats.

THE ASIA'S LEGACY
Though the Asia foundered in a storm, public outcry forced the Canadian Government to commission a hydrological survey of the Great Lakes' rocks and shoals. The charts from this survey are still used by mariners today.

ONE OF TWO SURVIVORS
Seventeen-year-old Christy Ann Morrison testified at the inquiry that the Asia had foundered because of the storm, not because of a shoal as some had thought.

Two Teenage Survivors

Asia Founders on Georgian Bay, Lake Huron

September 14, 1882

Built in 1873, the *Asia*, 136 feet (40.8m) long and 23 feet (6.9m) abeam, was designed specifically with a shallow, narrow hull to fit through the locks of the Welland Canal. Many argue that, in light of its dimensions, the steamer should never have been put into service on the treacherous open waters of Georgian Bay.

There was a storm warning in effect when Captain John Savage and the *Asia* left Owen Sound a little after midnight on September 14. The ship was grossly overloaded with cargo, including draft horses and cattle, on the main deck, as well as extra passengers sleeping on couches and chairs because of a scarcity of staterooms.

At Presque Isle the *Asia* took on a full load of cordwood fuel then headed north for the French River, away from the shelter of the Bruce Peninsula. The passengers had endured a difficult ride on the mounting seas, and presumably the captain was hoping that the load of fuel would improve the vessel's sickening roll. Hit by the full force of the gale, the *Asia* slowed to a crawl as the wheelsman tried desperately to keep the ship's nose into the wind to avoid the deadly troughs between waves.

By 9 a.m. the storm had reached a feverish height and the crew, in an effort to stabilize the pitching vessel, cut loose the cargo on deck and forced the horses overboard but within two hours, the wheelsman had lost the battle and the *Asia* fell into the troughs. Each wave threatened to capsize the ship and finally, she rolled completely over, tossing cargo and passengers into the roiling water.

Struggling not to drown, two teenagers, Dunkan Tinkiss and Christy Ann Morrison, found their way into one of the few lifeboats. A large group clung to the gunwales as the small boat flipped and tossed in the waves. After the storm calmed, only six of the lifeboat passengers, including the *Asia*'s first mate and Captain John Savage, remained. Following days of drifting aimlessly, all on board succumbed to exposure except the teenagers. Drifting onward with their grisly cargo, Tinkiss and Morrison finally landed on an island off Pointe au Baril where they were rescued by an Ojibwa couple. They were the only survivors of the *Asia*'s 122 passengers and crew.

TWISTED STEEL

The "Soo" Express was going full speed when it traveled onto the bridge over the Spanish River. The locomotive and the first second-class car made it across the bridge but the next car was off the tracks and it split in two; one half burst into flame, the other plummeted to the river, pulling the others cars with it.

SPANISH RIVER
TRAIN DERAILMENT

Webbwood, Ontario

JANUARY 21, 1910

On January 21, 1910, as the "Soo" Express, westbound from Montreal to Minneapolis, moved onto the cantilever bridge spanning the frozen Spanish River north of Sudbury, something went wrong. William Dundas, who was working in the express car, felt the cars pulling behind him in "a very ragged manner" Realizing the train was off the rails, he jumped. The rear wheels of the leading second-class coach had derailed first and it was dragged across the bridge with its passengers unharmed. The next coach derailed, smashed into a girder, and broke into two pieces; one piece nose-dived off the bridge and vanished under the ice, the other burst into flames. The first-class coach also came off the tracks and plummeted into the river. The diner car rolled down the embankment, its front half smashing through the ice.

Conductor Thomas Reynolds was in the diner car enjoying lunch when the accident occurred. He searched frantically for an exit and saw that the only way out was through a submerged door at the front of the car. Reynolds managed to swim through the door, but as he came to the surface he hit ice. Fighting the urge to breathe, he eventually found an opening and crawled onto the surface. Though bleeding from a head wound, he worked to get the rest of the passengers out. Using an ax to chop a hole in the car, he was able to pull out seven people alive.

Although accounts differ, most agree that 43 of the approximately 100 passengers died in the accident. The inquest jury was unable to determine the cause of the derailment.

ENGINEERING FAILURE

Forty-three people were killed when the cars plunged off the bridge into the frozen Spanish River.

BODIES FROM THE *WEXFORD*
Members of the steamer's 16-man crew washed ashore near Goderich, Ontario, after the Gales of November 1913.

THE BIG BLOW

Great Storm of 1913

NOVEMBER 7-10, 1913

Belying its reputation as a month famous for winter storms and high seas, November 1913 began unusually warm and calm, but before the month was out the worst storm in the history of Great Lakes maritime navigation would claim numerous ships and even more lives.

On November 7, 1913, a massive low-pressure system moved into Lake Superior from the Prairies, colliding with another low-pressure system moving north from Minnesota. Hurricane-force winds and driving snow buried towns and cities. Rail traffic ground to a halt and telegraph lines fell, leaving many towns isolated for days.

On November 8, a third low-pressure system originating in the Gulf of Mexico joined this icy maelstrom. No one was prepared for the violence that followed. On Lake Huron, the cruel combination of savage seas and blinding snow and ice made survival for any ship caught on the lake almost inconceivable.

When the *James Carruthers* left the dock at De Tour, Michigan at 12:53 a.m. on Sunday the 8th, two lanterns were clearly displayed, white above red, denoting a northwest storm warning. Such signals were a common sight in November, however, and usually ignored. In fact, owners often reprimanded any skipper who took shelter from such a storm, especially when other boats made port safely.

Several boats were beating north on Lake Huron: the tramp steamer *Wexford* loaded with grain, the *Howard M. Hanna, Jr.* loaded with soft coal and the 269-foot (81m) package freighter *Regina*. As the *Hanna* neared Harbor Beach, Michigan, the wind shifted briefly to the southeast, then to the northeast, and finally to the north-northeast, where it steadily increased in strength. By afternoon, it had begun to snow heavily and the ships struggled with limited visibility.

MANY FUNERALS
Many towns around the lakes were tied to the shipping industry and were devastated by the Big Blow, which took the lives of 235 sailors from these communities.

One of the first victims was the coal-laden *Argus*. When spotted by Walter C. Iler, captain of the steamer *George C. Crawford*, the *Argus* was struggling in murderous troughs. Then before Iler's eyes the worst possible scenario unfolded —the *Argus'* bow and stern sat atop two different waves and the cargo, heavy in the midships, was suspended between them. "The *Argus* just appeared to crumple like an eggshell and disappeared!" All hands were lost.

The next to be overcome was the *Hanna*. Around 8 p.m. a massive wave broke over the stern,

SHORELINE DEBRIS
Life belts bearing the names of foundered ships such as the Wexford, London *and* Carruthers *washed ashore.*

propelling the steward's wife and furniture from her room through an interior bulkhead, dropping them into the engine room, much to the astonishment of Chief Engineer Charles Mayberry. By 10 p.m. the *Hanna* was aground on the Port Austin reef, broken in two pieces.

Everywhere, vessels struggled to find safe ports. By late Monday the 5th, the storm had begun to ease and evidence of shipwrecks began to appear along the shores of Lake Huron. At Port Franks, 30 miles (48km) east of Port Huron, ten frozen crewmembers of the *Regina* were found, surrounded by debris and cargo: hay, canned goods and mixed freight. Two more were found nearby, frozen in a lifeboat.

A telegram received by the Pioneer Steamship Company in Cleveland confirmed that the *John A. McGean* had been lost with all hands. Three bodies lashed to a lifeboat bearing this name were found on the shore five miles south of Goderich, Ontario. The *Carruthers* was also presumed lost when life preservers, oars, and rudders were discovered. South of Goderich near Kincardine, bodies and wreckage from the *Argus* turned up.

Families began to arrive at the ports to identify bodies of their loved ones. In Hamilton, Thomas Thompson received a wire from his daughter Mrs. Edward Ward of Sarnia, reporting that his son had been drowned and he was to come to Goderich at once. Mrs. Ward was certain that her brother John Thompson had been on the wrecked *Carruthers*. Late Tuesday night, Thompson arrived and

THE PORT HURON TIMES-HERALD
EXTRA
PORT HURON, MICHIGAN, WEDNESDAY, NOVEMBER 12, 1913 — 10 PAGES TODAY — PRICE TWO CENT

10 BODIES FOUND
ALL FROM THE STR. REGINA
LOST BOAT IS NOT JENKS

identified one of the bodies as his son. The body's left forearm was tattooed with the initials "J.T."

The next day, John Thompson read of his own demise in a Toronto newspaper and immediately set off for Hamilton. For some reason, he did not send any word to his family. In the meantime, his father had purchased a cemetery plot and made arrangements for the funeral. When John arrived, the wake was in full swing. Thomas Thompson, utterly shocked by his son's appearance, exclaimed, "It's just like you to come back to attend your own wake, and you can get right out of the house until this thing blows over!"

At Port Huron early on Monday the 9th, while surveying the wreck of his life-saving station, Captain George Plough glanced at the murderous lake and spotted a dark object about 100 feet (30m) long, floating three miles (4.8kms) from shore. At first it was thought that it was the *Regina*, as crewmembers had been found not far from Port Huron. The hull lay in international waters between Canada and the United States but neither country immediately sent authorities to determine the ship's identity. The U.S. finally dispatched the cutter *Morrill*, but upon arrival at the site, the ship was ordered to turn around to assist the steamer *G. J. Grammer*, driven ashore on Lake Erie. Many were confounded by this decision as the hull, lying directly in the shipping lane, was a potential hazard.

William Livingstone, president of the Lake Carrier's Association, was enraged and dispatched the tug *Sarnia City* to investigate. The tug's crew speculated that the hull was stuck on the bottom of the lake, held by its spar. However, the hull could not be identified and Plough's discovery was dubbed the "mystery ship." Superintendent Dugan of the Merchant's Mutual Line Company, owners of the *Regina*, visited the wreck and declared it was decidedly not their ship. All reports were going to President Livingstone of the Lake Carrier's Association including that of the captain of the *Sarnia City*, who informed him that the mystery hull had eight plates, each no bigger than five feet (1.5m) across, indicating a vessel of between 250 and 300 feet (75-90m). Livingstone confidently announced that all American vessels of this size were accounted for and so the ship must be from Canada.

BODIES FOUND
(Left) Headline from the Port Huron Times-Herald. *(Above) The 269-foot (81m) package freighter* Regina.

Might it be the 250-foot (75m) steel bulk freighter steamer *Wexford*? A landowner near St. Joseph had made a particularly haunting discovery. A quarter mile offshore, a man seemed to be waving to him. It turned out to be a crewmember from the *Wexford*. His upraised arms were frozen stiff and as the body bobbed up and down, it appeared to be waving. Other crewmen were found on the beach, which was awash with grain from the *Wexford*'s hold. The *Wexford*, at about 250 feet (75m), could fit into Livingstone's theory.

First Mate James McCutcheon had been scheduled to sail on the *Wexford* but had missed his train. Now he was being called upon to identify the bodies of his friends. He admitted that it was the third time he had missed the boat and each time a disaster had occurred. In the first instance, the *Wexford* had caught fire and several lives had been lost. The second time there had been a wreck but the boat had been repaired. Although horrified by the task before him, he could not help declaring, "I'm the luckiest man alive!"

Milton Smith also considered himself lucky. He was an engineer on the missing *Charles S. Price*, but a strange premonition had kept him from sailing on what would be the *Price*'s last voyage. In Cleveland, Smith had been reading a newspaper to pass the time and was constantly drawn back to the weather forecast. There was no warning of anything unusual but Smith had a dreadful hunch. He repeated his fears to the chief engineer, John Groundwater, who scolded him for being foolish. Later, when Smith was called to Thedford to assist in the identification of his crewmates' bodies, he positively identified John Groundwater. This puzzled the coroner as the body had been found wearing a *Regina* life jacket. How did the Chief Engineer of the *Price* end up wearing a life jacket from the *Regina*?

Numerous other *Price* crewmembers were also found with *Regina* life jackets. The discovery of the *Price*'s cook with his apron still on seemed to suggest that

BURYING THE DEAD

A funeral procession makes its way through Goderich, Ontario, on the shore of Lake Huron.

EXTRA THE PORT HURON TIMES-HERALD.

PORT HURON, MICHIGAN, SATURDAY, NOVEMBER 15, 1913   12 PAGES TODAY   PRICE TWO CENTS

BOAT IS PRICE
DIVER IS BAKER
SECRET KNOWN

the ship had gone down quickly and at some point, the *Regina* must have foundered as neither hull has ever been found. Did the two ships collide in the storm?

Meanwhile, William Livingstone, who was still eager to positively identify the "mystery ship," received a call from Sarnia. The services of a professional diver and the tug *Sport* were available. Livingstone was overjoyed and cried, "For God's sake, get them if you can." The dive was set for Friday morning.

Unfortunately, because of rough seas the dive was called off until the following morning. As they waited, more bodies washed ashore near the Point Clark lighthouse, adding to the tension. Finally, on Saturday morning, six days after the discovery of the wrecked vessel, William Baker made his dive. He descended into the inky water and brought back the answer. "I read the name twice and then once more to be absolutely sure. The name was painted in black letters on white bulwarks—*Charles S. Price.*"

At Port Sanilac on Lake Huron a historical marker tells the story of the Great Storm of 1913:

> Sudden tragedy struck the Great Lakes on November 9, 1913, when a storm whose equal veteran sailors could not recall left in its wake death and destruction. The grim toll was 235 seamen drowned, ten ships sunk, and more than twenty others driven ashore. Here on Lake Huron all 178 crewmen of the eight ships claimed by its waters were lost. For sixteen hours gales of cyclonic fury made men and his machines helpless.

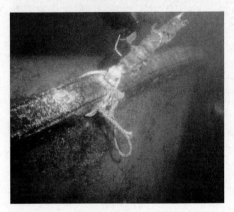

THE *PRICE* MYSTERY

(Top right) Composite of the Charles S. Price, *an overturned hull that went unidentified for six days. (Top left) The local newspapers followed the story of the mystery hull closely. (Above) Decades later, the hull of the* Price *sits in between 40 and 60 feet (12-18m) of water.*

PIG BOATS

*Whaleback freighters were designed to sit low in the water and were some-
times called "pig boats" by their crews because of the dank, dark quarters.*

GONE MISSING

The *Clifton* is Lost Northeast of Oscoda, Michigan

SEPTEMBER 22, 1924

The *Clifton* was a 308-foot (92m) steel whaleback bulk freighter, originally launched as the *Samuel Mather* at Superior, Wisconsin, in 1892. Whaleback freighters, sometimes called "pig" boats, were designed to sit low in the water and as such, they were not the favorites of crewmembers who were confined below decks without portholes.

On Saturday, September 20, 1924, the captain of the *Clifton*, Emmet D. Gallagher, was trying to load 2200 tons of crushed stone at Sturgeon Bay, Wisconsin, but was short of crew. The freighter had recently been converted to a self-unloader that despite the name required more men, not fewer, to operate. Gallagher ordered the chief engineer to round up the necessary crew and so when the *Clifton* left Sturgeon Bay, there were 27 men aboard.

The *Clifton* passed the Old Point Mackinac light and turned to the southeast. The captain was hoping to reach the Birmingham Sand & Stone Company dock in Detroit by late Monday afternoon. Conditions were not unusual when they put out into Lake Huron despite a strong southwest wind and building seas, but by late Sunday afternoon, the storm had strengthened to a ferocious gale.

By noon on Wednesday, the *Clifton* had failed to arrive in Detroit. No distress calls had been received and the last sighting had been on Sunday morning off Forty Mile Point. Nor had the vessel taken shelter in any of the harbors along the eastern shore. So what happened?

September 28, the steamer *Glencairn* came across a wreckage field and slowed to fish debris out of the lake. They found the broken remnants of the *Clifton's* pilothouse with the ship's clock pointing to 4 o'clock. The hull, however, has never been positively identified and is likely located somewhere northeast of Oscoda, Michigan.

WHALEBACK INVENTOR

Alexander MacDougall invented the whaleback, first launched in 1887. Although there was skepticism at first, the whalebacks became known for their seaworthiness.

FINALLY RESCUED
Five survivors picked up by the crew of the Manitoba *after spending three days in a life raft.*

DR. MIDDLEBORO
Arthur Middleboro, the purser on the Manasoo, managed to survive the foundering.

CARGO OF CATTLE
The Manasoo *was hired to take 100 head of cattle from West Bay to Owen Sound—it never reached its destination.*

FOUNDERING OF THE *MANASOO*

Georgian Bay, Lake Huron

SEPTEMBER 15, 1928

The 178-foot (53m) twin-screw passenger steamer *Manasoo* left West Bay on Manitoulin Island with a rather unusual cargo—100 head of cattle destined for Owen Sound. At 8 p.m. on September 14, the ship passed Little Current and headed out into Georgian Bay with no indication of problems ahead.

However, as so often happened on Lake Huron, by the time the *Manasoo* had reached Cape Croker, the southeast wind had turned into a full gale. Captain McKay headed towards Griffith Island to try and reach the shelter of Owen Sound Bay. The boat pitched, listing unnaturally as water streamed into the engine room. Only a short distance from Griffith Island, the *Manasoo* suddenly rolled over completely.

The purser, Arthur Middlebro, who had been thrown into the churning water, spotted something dark, which he reasoned to be two of the cattle. Maybe he could ride to the safety of Griffith Island on the back of one of them! Even more fortunately, it was a life raft. Six men, including Middlebro and Captain McKay, climbed aboard. Over the next three days the men suffered with scorching days and cold, windy nights. One of them died on the morning of the 17th, only hours before the *Manitoba* spotted them. Fifteen other crewmembers perished and were never found.

The unnatural list of the *Manasoo* led many to speculate that a steel plate had given way in the storm. Others contended that the cattle were improperly loaded and were loose on the deck, but McKay denied the accusations.

KEN MCCOLMAN WITH HIS OLD DIVE GEAR

Ken McColman was hired by victims' families to dive on the wreck to recover bodies. The ship was pitch black and McColman couldn't see the cow carcasses floating inside. He feared their horns might puncture the air-supply hose to his divesuit.

ONLY ONE SURVIVED
The 587-foot (176m) steel bulk freight steamer Daniel J. Morrell *now lies about 16 miles (25.5km) due north of Point Aux Barques, Michigan. Dennis Hale was the lone survivor.*

DANIEL J. MORRELL

BETHLEHEM
TRANSPORTATION
CORPORATION

DANIEL J. MORRELL SPLIT IN TWO

North of Point Aux Barques, Michigan

NOVEMBER 29, 1966

Determined that this would be his last season on the lake, Dennis Hale boarded the 587-foot (176m) steel bulk freight steamer *Daniel J. Morrell* on Monday, November 28, 1966, at Detroit. The boat was heading to Taconite Harbor, Minnesota, on Lake Superior to load a cargo of iron ore.

The weather report for Lake Huron that day was severe, and as the *Morrell* and her sister ship, the *Edward Y. Townsend*, left the St. Clair River, they faced the full force of a mounting storm. Winds reached 65 mph (104kph) and waves topped 25 feet (7.5m).

Hale came off watch at 8 p.m. and soon after lay in his bunk listening to the thuds and groans of the pitching *Morrell*. Suddenly he was jarred by a hard thump. The lights went out and the emergency bell began ringing. He ran on deck just as the boat began to crack in two. As the bow dove under the water, he and several shipmates managed to climb into one of two pontoon lifeboats on the forward section.

"The stern, still powered by its engines, was facing us and it started to run into the bow section, ramming us in the side." The force of the blow threw the crew into the water. Only four men, including Hale, made it back to the raft and they watched in amazement as the stern of the *Morrell* ran untamed across the lake.

When the men were finally spotted by a helicopter 36 hours later, the rescuers were astonished to see one of the men wave. Hale greeted them with "I love ya!" Twenty-nine men had been on board the *Morrell*. Three men in the raft had died of exposure. Hale was the only survivor.

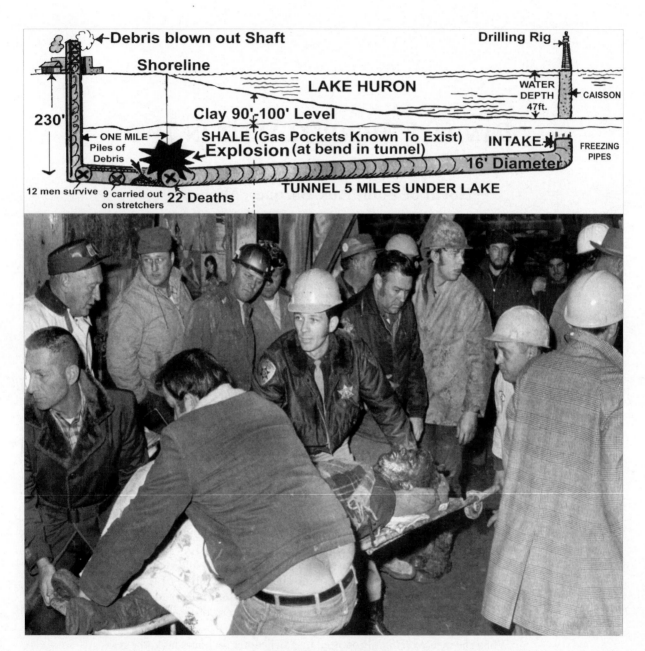

Debris blown out Shaft

Drilling Rig

Shoreline

LAKE HURON

WATER
DEPTH
47ft. ←CAISSON

230'

Clay 90'-100' Level

ONE MILE **SHALE (Gas Pockets Known To Exist)** **INTAKE**

Piles of
Debris **Explosion** (at bend in tunnel) FREEZING
PIPES

16' Diameter

12 men survive 9 carried out **22 Deaths** **TUNNEL 5 MILES UNDER LAKE**
on stretchers

ANATOMY OF A BLAST

(Top) Diagram shows where the explosion occurred in the water intake tunnel under construction. Over a 15-month period there were eight occasions when high levels of methane gas halted tunneling. (Bottom) Rescue workers bring a worker out on a stretcher.

Detroit Metropolitan Water System Tunnel Explosion

Port Huron, Michigan

December 11, 1971

On the afternoon of Saturday, December 11, 1971, an explosion ripped through a water intake tunnel under construction about 230 feet (69m) below the surface of Lake Huron near Port Huron, Michigan. The force of the blast was so immense that it ripped the 48-inch (120cm) corrugated metal air ducts to shreds, leaving a contorted mass of debris blocking the passageway and cutting off any escape for some of the workers further in the tunnel. Luckily, Eldon Bright was working near the elevator shaft and was one of the first to be lifted to safety. "You couldn't see because all the lights were knocked out. I don't know, maybe about 28 guys were trapped at the other end.... Sure they will bring them up eventually, but a lot of them are going to be dead."

It took rescue crews until 7 p.m. to reach the trapped men. Twice the rescuers had to be evacuated because of dangerous levels of methane gas. Ambulance worker Daniel Eastwood described the scene: "When we found men alive, we bandaged them, tied them to a stretcher and then moved on.... They would cry for us not to leave...." Some 40 workers were in the tunnel at the time of the blast; 21 were killed and 9 injured.

Investigations proved inconclusive but many believe that a crew working on the Lake Huron end of the tunnel five miles (8km) away set off the blast when they were drilling a ventilation shaft. Investigator Lindsay Hayes contended that a large drill bit broke loose, fell into the tunnel and set off sparks that ignited the methane gas.

The water tunnel, which was designed to carry fresh drinking water from Lake Huron to Detroit, was completed in 1974 and is capable of pumping 800 million gallons of water per day.

EXPLOSION TWISTS METAL
The force of the explosion was so great that it shredded the metal air ducts.

79

LAKE ERIE

HIGH SEAS
Waves wash over the deck of the William H. Truesdale *on Lake Erie. When squalls rise quickly, Erie's shallow waters can be deadly.*

EXPLOSION DOWNS *ERIE*

The steamship Erie *burned to the waterline and sank on August 9, 1841. When the remains of the burned-out hull were raised years later, they reportedly contained over $200,000 in gold and silver.*

EXPLOSION

Erie burns off Silver Creek, New York

AUGUST 9, 1841

On the evening of August 9, 1841, the wooden sidewheel steamship *Erie* moved easily through the calm water of Lake Erie, six miles (9.9km) from the port of Silver Creek, N.Y. There was a full complement of passengers on board: mostly Swiss and German immigrants, who carried with them their life savings and dreams of prosperity in the West. The deck was littered with wagon wheels, cradles, kitchen goods, and farm implements for their new homes.

Captain T.J. Titus was in the pilothouse when an explosion shook the deck. As he looked aft, he saw flames licking the ship's twin smokestacks and he watched in horror as the fire raced towards the stern. Titus tried to reach the ladies' cabins where the life preservers were stored but the heat drove him back.

On the main deck there was mass confusion. One survivor remembered:

> The air was filled with shrieks of agony and despair... The boat was veering toward the shore, but the maddened flames now enveloped the wheelhouse, and in a moment the machinery stopped. The last hope had left us... At this moment the second engineer...who had stood by his machinery as long as it would work, was seen climbing the gallows head, a black mass, with flames curling all around him. On either side he could not go...He sprang upward, came to the top, one moment felt madly around him, and then fell into the flame.

The most likely cause of the explosion was demijohns of turpentine and varnish that painters had carelessly placed on deck immediately above the ship's boilers. The workmen had just finished painting and varnishing the deck the evening before and were catching a ride to their next job in Erie, PA.

Twenty-nine people survived the tragedy and consensus places the death toll between 175 and 250.

G.P. Griffith in Flames

Articles from the wreckmaster's book of items recovered from the beach: 1 fiddle bow, 16 odd shoes, 10 bonnets, all worthless, 4 clothes brushes, 1 pocket flask, 27 cotton handkerchiefs, 1 snuff box, 19 hats, 35 caps.

Hoping for a Better Life

Thousands of immigrants traveled by steamship on the Great Lakes.

FIRE ABOARD THE *G.P. GRIFFITH*

Off the shore of Willoughby Township, Ohio, Two Miles (3.2km) West of the Chagrin River

NIGHT OF JUNE 16-17, 1850

As was the case with many passenger steamship disasters on the Great Lakes, the *G.P. Griffith* was overcrowded when it departed from Buffalo on Sunday, June 16. At Fairport, Ohio, two more passengers joined the many immigrants on board. Soon after, one of them, Stephen Woodin, reported to Mate William Evans that he smelled smoke. Evans swore at Woodin and told him to mind his own business. Woodin thought the mate was drunk, but went on his way without alerting anyone else.

Two miles (3.2km) out of Fairport, Wheelsman Dick Mann reported sparks reaching up between the smokestack and the roof of the cabins. Mate Sam McCoit desperately poured buckets of water into the opening but could not extinguish the flames. He ordered Mann to steer for shore and then sounded the alarm. The passengers, bleary-eyed and half-clothed, stumbled on deck while Chief Engineer Stebbins, finding the engine room already consumed by flames, pushed the throttles to full ahead and yelled to the engineer and fireman to quit their posts.

A half-mile (0.8km) from shore the *Griffith* struck a sandbar and came to a grinding halt. The passengers, relatively calm until now, began to panic. The two lifeboats were gone—their ropes burned through—and so a stream of people jumped over the side. Captain Roby, his wife and two children joined them (none of the family would survive). Others, fearing the water more than the flames, burned to death on deck.

Of an estimated 281 to 327 passengers, only 31 would survive. One was a five-year-old boy who was pulled from the water by a local fisherman. He was presumed dead, but on the beach, a local resident saw his lips move and quickly shook him by his heels to empty his lungs of water. The boy made a full recovery, but tragically he was the only one from his family to survive.

In the next few days, hundreds of bodies were washed ashore. A mass grave was dug to bury the many unidentified immigrants who perished. Ten days after the disaster more bodies showed up on the beach. All were German men, weighted down by their money belts, called "prosperity anchors," which had carried their dreams for new homes in the American West.

COLLISION ON LAKE ERIE

(Left) With the steam whistle broken, the Ogdensburgh's first mate shouted a warning to the Atlantic. No one heard his desperate cries and the ships collided.

CROWDED DECKS

(Lower) The Atlantic was hopelessly overcrowded, a common condition on steamships of the time whose owners collected as much money as possible by over-loading their ships with immigrants desperate to reach new homes in the American West.

THE COLLISION AND THE LAWSUIT

Atlantic and *Ogdensburgh*
Collide at Long Point, Ontario

AUGUST 20, 1852

On August 20, 1852, the *Atlantic*, a 267-foot (80m) sidewheeler, headed across Lake Erie bound for Detroit with over 600 passengers although it had been designed for only 200. Across the lake, the brand-new *Ogdensburgh* powered towards Buffalo with a cargo of wheat. First Mate Degrass McNell saw the Atlantic in the distance and prepared to yield to the other ship. When the ships neared, however, McNell reported that the Atlantic suddenly changed course. He immediately called the engine room to reverse engines and ran to the hurricane deck to shout a warning to the *Atlantic*. No one heard his desperate cries and the two vessels collided violently. McNell quickly checked the damage and determined it was safe to reverse away from the *Atlantic*. There did not seem to be much cause for alarm, for the *Atlantic* was back on course quickly. In fact, the *Ogdensburgh's* bow had punctured a gaping hole in the port side of the *Atlantic*. The ship was rapidly taking on water and within minutes it had reached the boiler room, dousing the fire in the engines, and bringing the *Atlantic* to a standstill. More than 300 panic-stricken passengers began to throw themselves overboard without first making any preparations for survival in the water.

As the *Atlantic* sank lower, the stern remained above the surface, buoyed by air trapped in the hold. About 250 passengers would cling there until rescued by the *Ogdensburgh*. Reports indicate that between 130 and 250 people perished.

Soon after the steamer went down, the American Express Company, who owned the vessel, hired John Green to recover the purser's safe. He found it on his second dive and secured it with a line. While preparing to lift the safe, a horrific pain tore through his chest and he lost feeling in his lower body in what was a near-fatal case of the bends. Five months later Green went back to the dive site only to find that his line was gone. Another diver, Elliot Harrington, hearing of Green's failure, had recovered the fortune, but after a court battle had to split the money with the American Express Company.

DIVER RECOVERS FORTUNE

Elliot Harrington had raided the wrecked Atlantic *and recovered $37,700. News of his find reached the owners, the American Express Company, who went to court to demand the money be returned. In the end Harrington had to split the money with them.*

ABIGAIL BECKER
AND HER MEDAL

(Top inset) Abigail Becker later in life, wearing the medal awarded to her by the Life-Saving Association of New York. (Lower inset) Close-up of medal. She received several awards for her bravery, including a signed letter from Queen Victoria.

DOOMED *CONDUCTOR*

The Conductor, a schooner similar to the one pictured here, was wrecked off Long Point, Ontario, where Abigail Becker spotted the crew clinging to the rigging in a November storm.

THE HEROINE OF LONG POINT

Long Point, Ontario

NOVEMBER 24-25, 1854

On a stormy November morning in 1854, Abigail Becker made her daily trip to the lake for water. As she neared the beach, she spotted an empty dinghy tossing in the surf. Then she saw the schooner *Conductor* with eight men clinging to the rigging beached several hundred yards offshore.

Abigail hurried back to her cabin to waken her older children. Together they made their way back to the beach and as the children gathered firewood, Abigail shouted encouragement to the seamen. The men had been clinging to the rigging since midnight, when their schooner ran aground. Although she could not swim, Abigail waded into the tumultuous water in an effort to convince the men to jump.

Captain Hackett was the first to cut himself loose and make for shore. As he neared the beach, his strength failed and he began to sink. Abigail pushed further into the crashing waves and dragged him to shore. Standing 6 feet (180cm) tall and weighing 215 pounds (97kg), she had immense strength. The mate was next to make the desperate swim. As he neared shore, he too faltered, and Abigail and the captain had to go back into the water to save him. Then, the captain, already weakened by his own struggle, began to flounder. Abigail had to haul both men back to safety! Four of the remaining crewmembers made the trip one by one, and each time Abigail waded out to snatch them before they slipped under the waves. Only one man remained on the doomed vessel. Frozen with fear, the cook could not brave the water. Abigail refused to give up hope and kept watch all night. The next morning the storm abated enough to let the captain, crew, and Abigail build a raft. Amazingly, the cook was still alive when they reached him.

Abigail's bravery was recognized several times, but no doubt her most prized memento was a signed letter from Queen Victoria, which reportedly contained a gift of fifty pounds.

STONE'S PET BRIDGE

Amasa Stone oversaw the design of the Ashtabula Bridge. The company engineer resigned his post because of a disagreement with Stone over the design.

HORRIFIC HOLIDAY SCENE

Snow falls on the burning Pacific Express, which fell through the bridge deck of the Ashtabula Bridge just after Christmas. A railroad employee sitting by the fire in his house heard the terrific crash and his wife rushed into the room saying, "My God, Henry; No. 5 has gone off the bridge!"

ASHTABULA BRIDGE COLLAPSE

Ashtabula, Ohio

CHRISTMAS 1876

Bridge building in the latter half of the nineteenth century became a major enterprise, for the most part because of the expansion of railroads in North America. In 1840 William Howe patented the Howe truss, which introduced the use of iron rather than wood. As a result, a huge demand for iron bridges fostered intense competition between manufacturers, leading to somewhat questionable quality control. Compounding the issue was the too-common problem of untrained laborers being hired and supervised by men who had little more idea of how to build a bridge than they did. In the 1870s and 1880s more than 200 bridges collapsed in North America.

One of the most spectacular bridge disasters occurred in Ashtabula, Ohio, just after Christmas in 1876. En route from Chicago, the Pacific moved out onto the eleven-year-old bridge. Dan McGuire, who controlled the throttle of the lead locomotive, felt the bridge sag and drove full steam ahead in an effort to make it across. His locomotive reached the other side, but eleven cars and a second locomotive behind fell as the bridge crumbled. As the potbellied stoves used for heating spilled over, the cars burst into flames. One hundred and fifty-six people died on the spot or later of their injuries.

The incident was reported across the country and questions began to surface. *Harper's Weekly* asked, "Was the bridge, when made, the best of its kind, or the cheapest of its kind?" Investigators placed the blame with Amasa Stone (Howe's brother-in-law), who had overseen the design of a wrought-iron single span bridge using the Howe truss. The company engineer had disagreed with Stone over the design and resigned his post when Stone went ahead without his approval.

TRAGIC AFTERMATH

Chief engineer of the railroad, Charles Collins, tendered his resignation after the bridge collapse but it was not accepted. A few days later he committed suicide—the result of being blamed for the disaster by the public and the press.

PARENTS SEARCH FOR THEIR CHILDREN

The Lakeview Elementary School was located on E. 152nd Street in Collinwood, Ohio. A memorial garden on the grounds of Memorial School now occupies the site.

LAKEWOOD
ELEMENTARY SCHOOL FIRE

Collinwood, Ohio (suburb of Cleveland)

MARCH 4, 1908

Approximately 325 students and 9 teachers were in attendance at Lakewood Elementary School in Collinwood, Ohio, on the morning of March 4, 1908, when an overheated steam pipe sparked a fire under the front stairs of the school. The flames spread rapidly through the dry wood-work and by the time firefighters arrived, the school was engulfed in flames. Those who exited the building via the front stairs were safe but 172 children and 2 teachers, trapped inside at the rear exit, died. Reports claimed that the exit doors opened inwards and in their panic the children had pressed up against the doors, making it impossible to open them.

However, in 1938, the Cleveland Board of Education made a startling discovery. After the demolition of the burned school, a memorial garden had been built on the site. While rebuilding the pool in the garden, work-men unearthed the old foundation of the Lakewood School. Director of Schools James Brown decided to excavate the entire area and to reconstruct blueprints in hopes of learning about possible flaws in the original design.

Once the reconstruction was complete, the reason for the terrific loss of life in 1908 became obvious. The front and rear exits of the school were identical. Both had wooden stairs leading to a vestibule with two doors that, in fact, did swing outwards. Beyond these were the outer doors, which also opened outwards. At the time of the blaze, one of the inner doors at the rear exit was locked. In their panic, the children jammed up against it. In the ensuing chaos many suffocated while others died in the flames.

Today schools are built with wider vestibules, no locks on inner doors and panic locks on outer doors.

ILL-FATED CAR FERRY

(Above) There were no survivors to tell the story of the foundering of the Marquette & Bessemer No. 2. (Inset) Searchers found the ship's number 4 lifeboat with nine men inside, frozen like ice sculptures. The clothes of another man were also found. Speculation was that he stripped and leapt into the lake.

BODIES LINED UP

(Right) Wreckage from the ferry was found off Long Point, Ontario, and bodies of crewmembers were found 15 miles (24km) off Erie, Pennsylvania.

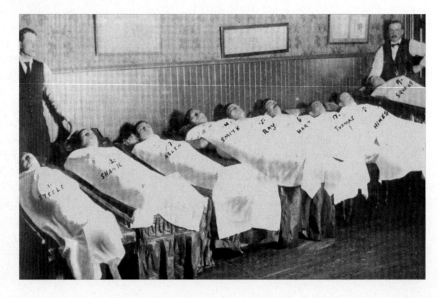

MARQUETTE & BESSEMER NO. 2 DISAPPEARS

Location unknown

NIGHT OF DECEMBER 7-8, 1909

The *Marquette & Bessemer No. 2* was built to ferry rail cars year-round on the sometimes treacherous water of Lake Erie. With its powerful engines and reinforced hull, the ship was one of the most seaworthy on the lakes. On the morning of December 7, 1909, the boat was scheduled to sail from Conneaut, Ohio, to Port Stanley, Ontario, with a full load of thirty railcars, filled with coal, steel and iron castings. As well there was a crew of thirty and one unusual passenger, Albert J. Weiss, treasurer of the Keystone Fish Company, who carried with him a suitcase filled with $50,000 in bills earmarked for the purchase of a Canadian fishing company.

The wind was mounting as the ship left the harbor sometime after 10:30 a.m., but there were no signs of an imminent storm. Later that day the temperature dropped to below freezing and by 5 p.m. the wind had reached 75 mph (120kph). Boats caught in the storm returned to port covered in thick layers of ice.

There is some dispute as to the course *Marquette & Bessemer No. 2* took that day. Varying reports put the vessel near Port Stanley and near Conneaut at the same time. Whatever the route, the *Marquette & Bessemer No. 2* was swallowed by the lake and never seen again.

One month before the boat's disappearance, Captain McLeod had complained of nearly losing the vessel in a storm when waves poured over the stern and into the cargo holds. The ship had been designed without a stern gate, but the owners promised to add one at the end of the season. Many speculate that the *Marquette & Bessemer No. 2* succumbed to the lake in exactly this way, but there were no survivors to verify any of the hypotheses.

To date, neither the hull nor Weiss' suitcase has been found—making the ship a favorite with treasure seekers.

CAPTAIN MCLEOD
McLeod had warned the owners that the open stern of the Marquette & Bessemer No. 2 *was susceptible to large waves. They promised to remedy the situation at the end of the season.*

CASUALTY OF THE STORM OF 1916

The whaleback freighter James B. Colgate *plummeted to the bottom of Lake Erie in an October storm in 1916. Captain Walter J. Grashaw was the only person to survive.*

BLACK FRIDAY!

Sinking of the *James B. Colgate*
off Long Point, Ontario

OCTOBER 20, 1916

October 20, 1916, marked one of the most tragic days in the history of Lake Erie navigation. Four vessels perished in a brutal storm: schooner *D. L. Filer*, lumber hooker *Marshall F. Butters*, the Canadian steamer *Merida*, and the whaleback freighter *James B. Colgate*.

Just after midnight, Captain Walter J. Grashaw directed the coal-laden *James B. Colgate* out of Buffalo harbor. Despite the rising wind and waves, he was not particularly concerned as the freighter had weathered 24 years on tempestuous Lake Erie. By dawn, the winds had risen to gale-force strength and the *Colgate* was increasingly at the mercy of the lake.

All day, waves crashed over the 302-foot (91m) freighter. Water poured into the hold faster than the pumps could spew it out and by 8 p.m. it was obvious the ship had little chance of survival. Shifting coal caused the *Colgate* to list. On the bridge, Captain Grashaw fruitlessly scanned the horizon for help.

Two hours later, the *Colgate* sank, nose first. The pounding waves had rid the deck of anything that could help the crew and all 26 men went into the water with only their life preservers to keep them afloat. Luckier than the others, Captain Grashaw, an engineer, and a stoker happened upon a raft that had been swept off the deck. They fought to keep the raft upright but twice it flipped over. Each time one man was lost. Only the captain remained. He survived on the raft for 35 punishing hours until the crew of the *Marquette & Bessemer No. 2* spotted him the next morning.

FIREFIGHTERS CLIMB TOWARDS VICTIMS

The Cleveland Clinic Foundation on Euclid Ave. at E. 93rd St. in Cleveland, Ohio, was founded by Dr. George Crile, Dr. Frank Bunts, Dr. William Lower and Dr. John Phillips, who, with the exception of Phillips, had served together in WWI. (Inset) As a result of the accident, new standards for the storage and manufacturing of nitrate film were developed.

THE CLEVELAND CLINIC DISASTER

Cleveland, Ohio

MAY 15, 1929

On the morning of May 15, 1929, Bofferty Bogg was called to investigate a leak in a basement room of the Cleveland Clinic. He uncovered a steam pipe, then left the room to have the main steam valve shut off. On his return he was shocked to discover a cloud of yellow smoke rising to the ceiling. He immediately grabbed a fire extinguisher and sprayed it towards the thick haze but was overcome by the fumes and fell to the floor. As he crawled towards the exit an explosion hurled him through an open door to where another workman was on duty. The two men quickly made their way to a window, then found themselves launched through the air and out of the building by another larger explosion.

The force of this second explosion lifted the roof off the clinic. Doors flew open and nurses and patients fled screaming from the building. On the second, third and fourth floors, hysterical patients and clinic staff trampled each other in the stairwells, crushing anyone who fell. Some managed to make it to open windows from which they leapt to safety but others were trapped when they could not break the glass.

There were many heroes that morning, including Ernest Stabb, an emergency policeman who repeatedly entered the building to save 21 people before being fatally overcome by the toxic fumes. Another was Robert Charles, a laborer at a nearby car wash who ran to the scene and held a ladder on his shoulders for ten terrified patients to climb down from a second storey window. Once they were safe, Charles raced into the building and pulled out ten more people.

One hundred and twenty-three people died in the disaster, including one of the clinic's founders, Dr. John Phillips. Investigators believe that x-ray film stored in the basement room where Bogg was working caught fire. Possibly the uncovered steam pipe was a factor in causing a toxic mixture of hydrocyanic acid and bromine gas to explode and spread throughout the building.

COMBING THE RUBBLE

The area affected by the gas explosion was bounded by East 55th Street, East 67th Street, St. Clair Avenue and the Shoreway. Every piece of fire equipment in Cleveland was pressed into service, supplemented by army, navy and Coast Guard personnel.

EAST OHIO GAS COMPANY EXPLOSION

Cleveland, Ohio

OCTOBER 20, 1944

On October 20, 1944, tank No. 4, containing millions of gallons of liquid natural gas, exploded at the East Ohio Gas Company Storage and Liquefying plant, scattering debris thousands of feet and turning a twenty-block area into a raging inferno.

Within minutes the tank next to No. 4 blew up and a stream of gas ran down the streets and into sewers, where it vaporized and found its way into the basements of hundreds of homes and businesses. The gases ignited, buildings exploded and the scene quickly came to resemble a battlefield. Birds fell from the sky, burned by the heat waves escaping upwards, and people ran screaming from the burning buildings.

Police drove through the area with sound trucks warning, "The neighborhood is on fire! Get out! Run eastward!" At the same time new explosions sent manhole covers spiraling into the air and water mains blew apart. Drivers fled their cars and joined the wave of people running towards the safety of Lake Erie.

By late afternoon most of the fire had burned itself out and hundreds of rescue workers began to comb the scarred area for survivors. The Red Cross set up shelters in schools, churches and meeting halls to house the fifteen hundred who were made homeless.

In its wake, the disaster left 130 people dead, including fifty employees of the East Ohio Gas Company, many of whom had tried to escape by hiding in metal lockers at the plant. Only their jewelry was left to identify them.

Investigators found no conclusive cause for the leak in tank No. 4, but a company spokesperson did report that a similar problem with the tank had been discovered and repaired soon after its delivery to the plant.

"It is unbelievable, fantastic"

A headline describing ambulances, fire trucks and police cars that lined Ouellette Avenue in downtown Windsor, Ontario, after an explosion at the Metropolitan Store. (Inset) A victim of the explosion with bandaged head and hand.

METROPOLITAN STORE EXPLOSION

Windsor, Ontario

OCTOBER 25, 1960

Passersby were stunned when a violent explosion rocked the Metropolitan store in downtown Windsor shortly after 2 p.m. on October 25, 1960. Merchandise, debris and people flew out the glass front window onto Ouellette Avenue. At the rear of the store an entire wall gave way. Bystanders rushed to help and emergency workers were on the scene within minutes. They concentrated their efforts in the basement where the store's lunch counter had dropped through the floor. An employee, Mrs. McMillan, who was in the store twenty minutes before the blast, reported that most of the 66 stools at the counter were full

On and off during the first few hours of the rescue operation, cries of "mama" could be heard, which spurred the workers to dig furiously in an effort to find the trapped "baby." No child was found. It was later discovered that the "baby" was really a doll that cried "mama" when squeezed.

The explosion had originated in the store's furnace room where workers were converting the furnace from coal to gas. Joseph Halford, the store manager, described what happened:

DESPERATE SEARCH
Rescue workers sift through the wreckage hoping to find more survivors.

> We had turned on the gas, but nothing came out but air.... A plumber's helper got a larger wrench and opened the five-inch valve from the main. More air rushed in and with it must have come some gas. We had a small summer heater burning in one corner of the room. I guess when the escaping gas hit that everything went. The roof fell in.

The explosion claimed ten adult lives and sent at least 65 injured to nearby hospitals.

HOW DID IT HAPPEN?
Investigators examine the plane for clues. (Inset) The MD-82 crashed into an embankment on I-94 in Romulus, Michigan.

MIRACLE ON FLIGHT 255

Northwest MD-82 Crashes After Takeoff at Detroit Metro Airport

AUGUST 16, 1987

At 8:43 p.m. on Sunday, August 16, 1987, Northwest flight 255 was cleared for takeoff from Detroit's Metro Airport. As the jet raced down the runway and rose into the air, Pilot John Maus' control column was vibrating madly and the plane was climbing slowly, rolling to the right. Suddenly it pitched left and a warning in the cockpit said, "Stall...stall...stall." The left wing clipped a light pole, tearing off part of the wing and leaking fuel into the engine, which burst into flames. After hitting another pole, the plane rolled 35 degrees, ground over a roof and crashed into an embankment. The forward 20 feet (6m) broke away and continued hurtling down the road in a mess of sparks and flying metal.

Within minutes rescuers were on the scene searching for survivors. Later, Jack Drake of the National Transportation Safety Board would say, "The plane was so compromised that the potential for survival was virtually nil." But one passenger was miraculously found alive under a seat. Four-year-old Cecelia Cichan would be the only survivor of the 149 passengers and 6 crew on board.

Investigators concluded that the crash was caused by a failure to extend the plane's wing flaps and slats during takeoff, a routine procedure that improves lift and handling. Why this was not done could not be determined from the cockpit recorder but it appeared that Maus and the first officer had neglected to go through the required pre-flight checklist and that the aural warning system, which should have warned that the flaps and slats were not extended, was not functioning.

SOLE SURVIVOR
Four-year-old Cecelia Cichan was pulled from the wreckage alive.

HOMES ABANDONED

By February 8, 1979, 899 homes were ordered evacuated. The Department of Justice filed suit against the Hooker Chemical Corporation on December 20, 1979, ordering the company to clean up four chemical waste dump sites in Niagara Falls. Barbara Blum of the EPA said, "Today's suit should serve notice to those who generate or handle hazardous waste that these kinds of dangers no longer will be tolerated by the American public."

THE LOVE CANAL

Niagara Falls, New York

FIRST EVACUATIONS AUGUST 1978

When residents in the La Salle section of Niagara Falls, New York, discovered chemical waste leaching into their neighborhood in the spring of 1978, the Love Canal Crisis began. However, the roots of the problem could be traced back to 1892 when William T. Love first proposed to dig a canal from the Niagara River in order to provide hydroelectric power for his planned industrial community, Model City. Love ran out of money and the project was never completed, leaving an excavation 60 feet (18m) wide and 3000 feet (900m) long. In 1920 the site was sold at public auction and between 1942 and 1953 was used primarily by the Hooker Chemicals and Plastics Corporation (now Occidental Chemical) to dispose of 22,000 tons of mixed chemical wastes such as lindane and DDT (both pesticides that have since been banned in the United States), multiple solvents, PCBs, dioxin and heavy metals.

In 1953 the landfill was closed, covered over with dirt, and deeded to the Niagara School Board. Houses sprang up around the landfill area and the 99th Street Elementary School was built to serve 400 students. From the late 1950s to the 1970s, there were occasional reports of unidentified substances coming to the surface and of strange odors in the area. The city would simply cover the offending substances over with dirt and clay but when heavy rain and snowfalls in 1975 and 1976 led to high groundwater levels, 55-gallon drums began to appear. Niagara Falls could no longer ignore the problem. They hired Calspan Corporation to investigate. Calspan found toxic chemical residues in the air and in many residential sump pumps at the south end of the canal, as well as high levels of PCBs in the storm sewer system. They recommended that the canal be capped with clay, that the sump pumps be sealed off and a drainage system be installed to control the migrating waste. Except for placing window fans in a few homes found to contain high levels of chemical traces, the city did virtually nothing.

In the spring of 1978, the local newspaper ran articles about the site, alerting residents to the fact that the canal had once been a chemical dump site. One concerned parent, Lois Marie Gibbs, requested that her son be transferred out of the 99th Street School because he had been continually sick since moving into the area. Her request was denied on the grounds that it would set a bad precedent, but Gibbs did not give up. She went to the School Board and

**LOIS MARIE GIBBS
AND DAUGHTER**

*(Above) Gibbs argues that
Carter's decision to evacu-
ate the Love Canal was
heavily influenced by public
pressure in an election year,
and that the "Love Canal
taught us that the government will only protect you
from such poisoning only
when you force it to."*

DEAF CHILD AREA

*(Right) This sign reveals
one of the effects attributed to the leaching of
toxic chemicals.*

to both her city and state representatives. No one
would help and so she went door to door in her neighborhood with a petition to close the school. She learned
that many more people were sick. Gibbs formed the
Love Canal Parents Parents Movement, which eventually grew into the Love Canal Homeowners
Association (LCHA).

Gibbs' petition was instrumental in bringing more
media attention to the crisis and angry residents forced the New York
State Department of Health to initiate environmental testing. In April
1978 Health Commissioner Robert Whalen declared the Love Canal
area a threat to human health and part of it was fenced off. On August
2, the Department of Health declared a state of emergency and recommended pregnant women and children under two be moved out of this
area. Less than a week later the mandate was expanded to include people of all ages and 239 families were evacuated. The State agreed to pur-
chase their homes and established the Love Canal Interagency Task
Force to coordinate the relocation of families, the continuation of stud-
ies and the construction of a drainage system to prevent further leaching
of toxic chemicals.

The cleanup began in October 1978. A drainage trench was dug
around the perimeter and a clay cap was placed over the landfill to
reduce the amount of water penetration. It did not, however, address
the problem of the chemicals that had already leaked into the neighborhood. The community was not satisfied, and so the State erected a
10-foot (3m) fence around the "affected" area. At the same time they
began to make public statements that there was no evidence of abnor-
mal health problems outside the fenced area.

The LCHA was furious. One of its surveys had uncovered problems
far outside the fence. With the help of volunteer scientist Dr. Beverly

Paigen, they began to interview families in the area. They plotted their data on a map and immediately it became apparent that the heath problems were clustered in specific developed areas where old streambeds had been covered up. Their results were startling and showed increases in miscarriages, still births, nervous breakdowns, hyperactivity, epilepsy and urinary tract disorders. When the LCHA presented its findings to the state heath authorities, they were dismissed. The community took to the streets in protest and thousands of concerned citizens wrote letters to the governor, to legislators and even the President of the United States. Under pressure, on February 8, 1979, the Department of Health issued a second evacuation order for another 660 families in the area.

On October 1, 1980, U.S. President Carter went to Niagara Falls to sign a bill authorizing funds to relocate any family that wished to leave the area. Members of the LCHA are convinced that if they had not organized to apply constant pressure, they would still be living in their toxic homes, with authorities still maintaining that the area was safe.

The Love Canal was one of the first crises of its kind to garner national attention and was instrumental in the passage of the Comprehensive Environmental Response, Compensation, and Liability Act, commonly known as the Superfund, passed by the United States Congress in December 1980. The Superfund provides funds from industry and the federal government to clean up hazardous waste sites where responsible parties cannot be determined or cannot afford to pay. In 1982, $7 million from the Superfund was committed to the cleanup of the Love Canal. Acting on behalf of the Environmental Protection Agency (EPA), the United States Department of Justice filed suit against the Hooker Chemical Corporation on December 20, 1979, ordering the company to clean up four chemical waste dump sites in Niagara Falls. The suits dragged on until June 1989 when the company signed a consent order to take over storage and destruction of wastes originating at the Love Canal site.

Two hundred thirty-nine homes in the Love Canal area were destroyed, but in September 1988, over two hundred homes were declared "habitable" and families began to move back into the area. By March 1998 Occidental Chemical (previously Hooker Chemical Corporation) had settled with the 2300 families who had sought damages from their time living near the Love Canal. By spring 1998 the company was completing construction of a system to remove and treat the polluted groundwater within the landfill cap and the cleanup is ongoing.

THE YOUNG VICTIMS
An LCHA study showed startling health problems in the Love Canal area. Fifty-six percent (9 of 16) of children born between 1974 and 1978 had birth defects such as three ears, a second row of teeth or developmental delay.

GREAT TORONTO FIRE, 1904
Downtown Toronto looking north up Bay Street from Front Street. Five thousand people were left jobless but miraculously there were no deaths.

Lake Ontario

PRIDE OF THE 34TH

The British sloop Ontario was located near Wilson, New York, by divers in 1995, partially buried in silt. Because of the deep, cold water, it is in excellent condition.

Royal Navy Sloop *Ontario* Lost

Near Wilson, New York

November 1, 1780

Built in May 1780 at the Carlton Island Shipyard, near the mouth of the St. Lawrence River, the *Ontario* was the pride of the British 34th Company. At 123 feet (37m) the sloop was the largest ship on the lakes at the time. Its military role was to prevent an American attack on Montreal by way of the Mohawk and St. Lawrence Rivers.

Soon after the *Ontario's* launch, the 34th Company learned that they would participate in an autumn raid to engage the rebel forces and to destroy crops destined for the American Army. The soldiers would join with other troops in Oswego, then travel east by whaleboat and on foot to Stone Arabia, located on the north shore of the Mohawk River.

At the end of September, the *Ontario* set out from Carlton Island. The raiding party was dropped at Oswego and plans were made for the *Ontario* to return to pick them up in late October. When the vessel set out from Niagara on its return trip there were about 120 passengers aboard: 37 men of the 34th Company travelling to garrison duty at Carlton Island, a few prisoners, four natives, a civil merchant, several other soldiers and several dependents of the men in the 34th.

Late afternoon on October 31, 1780, the *Ontario* was spotted about 30 miles (48km) east of Niagara sailing in a southwest wind. During the night it ran headlong into a sudden storm (some say a hurricane), which capsized the vessel and felled both masts, and eventually sent the sloop to the bottom of Lake Ontario. In the following July, six bodies from the *Ontario* surfaced about 12 miles (19km) east of Fort Niagara—the only ones ever found.

TAKEN BY A TEMPEST
Ontario *battles the storm that would eventually knock it over.*

TIME CAPSULES

The Hamilton and Scourge are two of the best surviving examples of warships from their era in the world and they have been declared World Heritage Sites by the United Nations. They rest in the deep, cold water of Lake Ontario near Hamilton, Ontario.

WARSHIPS *HAMILTON* AND *SCOURGE* FOUNDER DURING WAR OF 1812

Mouth of Niagara River

AUGUST 8, 1813

At the mouth of the Niagara River, near St. Catharines, Ontario, two wooden United States Navy schooners, the *Hamilton* and the *Scourge*, 112 feet (34m) and 110 feet (33m) respectively, lie upright in a bed of silt clay. Pristinely preserved by the dark, ice-cold water of Lake Ontario, they are considered to be two of the best examples of nineteenth-century warships extant in the world. Sabers still lie where the crews dropped them and skeletons litter the hulls.

Originally built as merchant ships the boats were pressed into service for the United States Navy during the War of 1812 with Great Britain. On the evening of August 8, 1813, the schooners dropped anchor at the mouth of the Niagara River. The enemy fleet lay anchored nearby. Many of the crew bunked down for the night on deck to be ready in the event of a night attack.

On the *Scourge*, Ned Myers was awakened by a sudden rush of wind and rain on his face. Before the sails could be hauled in, a squall hit the schooner and within minutes the *Scourge* keeled over and sank. Myers and some of his crewmates were thrown into the water but others less fortunate were trapped by loose guns sliding across the deck. Myers found the *Scourge's* tender, climbed aboard, and dragged seven other men to safety. In the pitch black they started to row, only catching glimpses of their surroundings in flashes of lightning, and hoping they would not blunder into the British fleet. Thankfully, they happened upon the American schooner *Julia* and were welcomed aboard. The captain immediately sent out a boat to search for other survivors. They found only four, all from the *Hamilton*—another victim of the squall!

Of an estimated one hundred men on board the two schooners, these twelve men were the only survivors.

Since 1971, the *Hamilton* and *Scourge* wrecks have been the subjects of numerous research projects that have generated hundreds of still photographs and hours of video footage.

BEFORE THE WAR
(Above) The Scourge *was launched as the Royal Navy schooner* Lord Nelson. *(Below) The* Hamilton *was a merchant ship called* Diana *before 1812.*

OXFORD BREAKS THROUGH

(Top left) Anxious to hear who had died, crowds gathered at the Great Western Depot in Hamilton as corpses were taken into one of the large baggage rooms. Sixty corpses were lain out in an out building adjoining the Station House. (Top right and Lower) Before the train reached the bridge, the axle of the right front locomotive wheel had fractured. By the time the train reached the bridge, the front locomotive was derailed and it drove through the bridge deck. Scores of volunteers walked along the tracks to the canal and worked through the night, lit by locomotive lamp and torchlight.

DES JARDINES CANAL
TRAIN WRECK

Near Hamilton, Ontario

MARCH 17, 1857

Steaming along the Great Western Railway between Toronto and Hamilton on March 17, 1857, the 23-ton locomotive Oxford approached the Des Jardines canal bridge, where two tracks merged. The railway employees at the switch waved the train through with its tender, baggage car and two first-class coaches.

Suddenly the cars were shaken by a violent jolt. Fearing for their lives, some of the passengers and crew jumped out of the moving train. As the Oxford drove onto the wooden bridge, there was a terrific crunching noise—the front wheels were off the track! The locomotive broke through the floor of the bridge and hurtled 50 feet (15m) to the ice-covered canal below, dragging the rest of the cars with it.

Of the approximately 90 people on board, 60 were killed (some accounts say 59). Most died immediately while others drowned in the icy water that poured into the coaches.

A coroner's inquest met for nearly a month to determine the cause of the accident. The Oxford was only 18 months old and there was no rust at the point where the right wheel had broken off. The question of the bridge was more contentious. While most engineers declared it to be in good repair, a few disagreed, including Frederick P. Ruthbridge of the Department of Public Works. He produced samples of wood rot that others had overlooked and contended the bridge was "in an unsound, impaired, and dangerous condition." A somewhat ambiguous compromise was struck in the final report. The bridge was pronounced to be safe, provided the railway cars remained on the track.

TRAIN PLUMMETS
Engineer Burnfield whistled once, apparently for brakes, then the locomotive Oxford broke through the bridge, pulling the tender, baggage car, and two first-class coaches after it.

ON TOP OF THE TELEGRAM BUILDING
Men look out over down-town Toronto, surveying the burned-out buildings. The Evening Telegram employees saved their building from the fire with hand-held hoses and were awarded a bonus by the owner.

THE GREAT TORONTO FIRE

Toronto, Ontario

APRIL 19, 1904

At 8:04 p.m. on April 19, 1904, two alarms rang out at the Lombard Street Fire Hall in downtown Toronto. Fire Chief John Thompson and his men hurried to the E.S. Currie Building on Wellington Street with a full arsenal: three horse-drawn engines, seven hose wagons, an aerial truck, water tower, and hook and ladder. They found the building beyond help and quickly realized that this was not their only concern. Strong winds threatened to carry the fire to the Gillespie-Ansley building next door.

With four of his men, Chief Thompson raced into the Gillespie-Ansley building but they were no match for the wind-blown fire. The building filled with smoke as flames leapt across the alley and the five men had to be evacuated through an upper floor window. During his descent, the chief slipped and hurtled three floors to the pavement, snapping his leg. He was rushed to hospital leaving his deputy, John Noble, to coordinate the fight.

At 8:51 p.m. Noble sounded the general alarm and every firefighter in Toronto was called in to combat the inferno. Just after 9 p.m. the front wall of the Davis and Henderson building at 84 Bay Street collapsed, sending showers of embers across the street onto the Evening Telegram and Office Specialty buildings. Although the Telegram was equipped with sprinklers, they failed, and the night shift was faced with the task of trying to save the building as windows exploded around them. With wet towels covering their heads and using only handheld hoses, they fought the fire without assistance for more than two hours. Their efforts saved the building and earned them a bonus from newspaper proprietor John Ross Robertson.

Firefighters were concentrating their efforts on the Office Specialty building, as they knew there was a real danger of the flames spreading north and east to King, Queen and Yonge Streets. By 9:30 p.m. they had

FIRE CHIEF JOHN THOMPSON
A broken leg early in the fire disabled the chief, leaving firefighters to battle Toronto's worst fire without their leader.

SURVEYING THE DAMAGE

From the Customs House looking west down Front Street. Firefighters set up a final defense in the alley between the Customs House and a burning warehouse. They were forced into the Customs House with their hoses, but managed to halt the flames. (Inset) A pail of nails fused by the intense heat.

managed to get this line of fire under control but the southern edge was in trouble. The fire had leapt across Wellington Street into the Brown Bros. Bookbinding and Stationery establishment (which contained excellent kindling!), then raged through the Rolph-Smith building next door. It quickly collapsed. Several firefighters were inside at the time, but they managed to escape unharmed. The fire crews were forced to retreat further south to Piper Street.

Unlike those at the Telegram, the sprinklers at the W.R. Block building on the southwest corner of Wellington and Bay Streets did activate properly but they were no match for the driving flames. By the time Toronto's mayor, Thomas Urquhart, arrived on the scene, the entire north side of Front Street was engulfed. He called for even more help and by 11 p.m. firefighters from as far away as Hamilton had joined the battle.

By this time thousands of spectators had collected to gawk at the incredible sight. The noise was deafening as walls crashed, windows exploded and live wires crackled when they fell into puddles of water. The flames had now bridged Bay Street and were racing eastward towards Yonge Streetæthe heart of the city.

Directly in the fire's path was the Queen's Hotel (where the Royal York Hotel now stands). But hotel management had a plan. They first sent all female staff with the hotel silver to other city hotels, then they immediately set to work to save the building. Every bathtub was filled with water and wet blankets were hung from every window shutter. The roof caught fire several times, but the staff was able to extinguish the flames. The only scars left by the fire were a scorched roof and some blistered paint.

As the fire progressed to the south and the east, firefighters and city officials decided to take drastic action. They would destroy any building lying directly in the path of the fire in order to create a firebreak. Military engineers were called in to do the blasting, but no dynamite could be found anywhere in the city.

Another approach was needed and so firefighters were positioned in the alley between the Customs House building on the south side of Front Street and a burning warehouse— the front line of the fire. At times the

flames came to within eight feet of the firefighters and some were driven, along with their hoses, into the Customs House. Thankfully their efforts were rewarded and the warehouse collapsed in a heap of embers around 4:40 a.m., stopping the relentless march of the blaze.

As morning dawned, a tremendous scar stretched across the middle of downtown Toronto. The smoldering area was a desolate waste and almost nothing was salvageable. Power lines were strewn across streets that were now just a mess of melted asphalt. The fire had ravaged more than 19 acres (7.7 hectares) and destroyed 98 buildings.

Miraculously, no lives were lost. The pre-fire optimism of the growing city wavered only momentarily. Toronto quickly returned to business. The 5,000 people left jobless soon found work elsewhere and it was reported that businesses even offered assistance to those rivals whose livelihoods had been destroyed.

At the time it was speculated that the conflagration was ignited by faulty wiring in the Currie building. The manager of the Toronto Electric Light Company strongly denied the accusations as the building had been inspected only four months earlier and been declared safe. Another rumor circulated that a stove used by employees working overtime had overheated, but the company vehemently denied this as well. Because of the severity of the fire, it was impossible to ascertain from the rubble what had actually happened and the cause remains a mystery.

PICKING UP THE PIECES

(Top) The cleanup lasted for several months. (Inset) Five thousand people were left unemployed by the fire but Toronto rallied around them and many were hired for the cleanup and rebuilding of Toronto's downtown.

WINTER SCENE
Mound at the base of the Falls shows the degree of ice accumulation the river can be subject to.

TOY BRIDGE
Piled ice created enough pressure to push the bridge off its abutments.

HONEYMOON BRIDGE COLLAPSE

Between Niagara Falls, Ontario
and Niagara Falls, New York

JANUARY 27, 1938

Because of the thousands of newlyweds who honeymooned in Niagara Falls, the Upper Steel Arch Bridge (which spanned the Niagara River gorge between Niagara Falls, Ontario, and Niagara Falls, New York) had been affectionately dubbed the "Honeymoon Bridge." In late January 1938, unusual weather conditions, thin ice on Lake Erie, and a five-day January thaw followed by three days of high winds led to a dangerous ice jam. Piles of ice had built up around the bridge abutments and by early morning on January 26, maintenance crews had been called out to tackle the problem but were forced to retreat because of rising water. By the 27th, the ice jam stretched from the river bottom to a height of 150 feet (45m), creating a virtual dam. Popping rivets could be heard as the bridge groaned under the strain. Similar ice conditions in 1899 had bent one of the bottom girders, but the bridge had since been reinforced several times.

"HONEYMOON BRIDGE"

The bridge linked Niagara Falls, New York, and Niagara Falls, Ontario, an area frequented by honeymooners.

Thousands of spectators, newspaper reporters and photographers were drawn to the scene. Douglas and Wesley Styles, 12 and 13, crept past the watchmen to get a picture of the spectacular chunks of ice. Suddenly, the bridge trembled as the moving ice pushed it off its abutments on the American side. The two boys ran out of the way just as the bridge crumpled. Then the entire section folded, pulling the Canadian side away from its anchorage. The once proud Honeymoon Bridge lay broken in four main sections on the frozen river, now a mass of twisted steel and wood.

In the spring, the bridge's wreckage was dynamited to break it into smaller pieces, which sank to the bottom of the river. Planning had begun for a new Honeymoon Bridge.

THE END OF AN ERA
Many historians note that the burning of the Noronic marked the end of luxury liners on the Great Lakes.

THE *NORONIC* IS BURNING

Toronto, Ontario

SEPTEMBER 17, 1949

BEFORE AND AFTER
The elegant dining room of the Noronic *was charred beyond recognition.*

The *Noronic* had a reputation. When the 362-foot (110m) cruise ship was built in Port Arthur in 1913 it was the largest of its kind on the lakes. One passenger recalled: "To sail her, gorge on steak in her elegant dining room and sip a cool drink while sunk into a wicker chair was an exercise in pure decadence. Getting there was never the point of a voyage aboard the *Noronic*." The vessel also enjoyed another sort of fame. It was common practice for well-to-do gentlemen to come aboard the *Noronic* accompanied by women other than their wives. Some would use different names to hide their activities, but it was well known among the crew and certain staterooms were reserved for these passengers. For this reason the *Noronic* earned the unfortunate nickname the "*Whoronic*." Its last voyage would mark the beginning of the end for Great Lakes cruise ships.

During the summer season the *Noronic* worked the Sarnia-Lakehead run, but each September the ship made two popular post-season cruises, picking up passengers in Cleveland and Detroit, heading through the Welland Canal to Lake Ontario, stopping in Toronto and then continuing on to the Thousand Islands. Just before 7 p.m. on September 17, 1949, the *Noronic* slipped into Toronto harbor, announced by a deep blast of the ship's whistle. The vessel berthed at Pier 9 for the night and many of the approximately 525 guests debarked to explore Toronto's nightlife. Captain William Taylor gave all but 15 of the 171 crewmembers the night off before departing himself.

Those passengers who stayed aboard did not lack for entertainment. Although the *Noronic's* bars were closed, many had their own supply of liquor. Clusters of passengers could be seen playing cards and generally amusing themselves while many

BETTER TIMES

The Noronic *in Detroit. The largest passenger ship on the Lakes was known for its stunning rooms such as the sunroom (inset).*

younger patrons enjoyed dancing to the ship's orchestra. By 1:30 a.m. the dancers began to drift away and most of the passengers had returned from their night on the town. They retired to their staterooms—many, it has been noted, far from sober.

A few minutes later three Detroit women, Mrs. Agnes Hintz, Mrs. Henry Hafeli and Mrs. John Slaninski, smelled smoke. Sensing possible danger, they calmly left the ship.

Josephine Kerr was travelling with her brother and sister-in-law and their children Kathleen (10), Barbara (6) and Philip (8). A friend of Captain Taylor's, Josephine had spent the evening at the home of friends with the captain. They arrived back on the *Noronic* at about 1:25 a.m. and Josephine returned to the stateroom she was sharing with the two Kerr girls. Soon after, the smell of smoke wafted under the door and Josephine immediately wakened the girls. The three hurried out of the room and ran to warn the other Kerrs. When no one responded to their repeated knocking they decided that they had already left and so they moved towards D deck where they were stopped by thick smoke that was already choking the ship's passageways. Somehow they made their way to an observation area on C deck where it became obvious that the only way to get off the ship was over the railing, which was 60 feet (18m) above the water. Kathleen climbed over the side first and started down a steel cable attached to the pier below. Halfway down, a woman above her slipped and knocked Kathleen into the water but she managed to swim to the pier. Six-year-old Barbara was next. A Cleveland

FIGHTING THE FLAMES

(Above left) Eighteen fire trucks, 1 fire-fighting boat, and fleets of police and ambulances arrived on the scene after the fire alarm was set off. Firefighters battled the blaze with ladders, pouring water onto the Noronic *for many hours after the fire was first discovered.*

CAPTAIN WILLIAM TAYLOR

(Above right) Captain Taylor had spent the evening with friends in Toronto. It was rumored he was less than sober on his return to the vessel, although he vehemently denied this charge.

man, Arthur Alves, put her on his back and made his way down the cable. (At a later reunion with the Kerrs, Alves admitted that his actions that night had caused trouble with his wife, who thought he was on a hunting trip.) Finally, Josephine jumped and safely made it to the pier. The other three Kerrs did not survive.

Elsewhere Mrs. Saul Kecti and Mrs. Max Peller were lucky enough to stumble across a gangway to the SS *Kingston*, which was sharing the slip with the *Noronic*. They were the last to leave this way, however, as the *Kingston* backed away from the *Noronic* when sparks and burning debris started to come down on the decks. Fueled by multiple layers of paint, the fire had quickly spread throughout the ship. Those on the starboard side (facing the water) were cut off from the gangways and had to decide between jumping into the lake or burning on deck. Because of the courageous efforts of civilians and rescue workers in various small craft, only one person drowned after making that frightening leap.

On the port side, some passengers ran to the crowded gangways while others climbed down ropes thrown over the side. In the panic to escape the flames, some acted only out of self-preservation. One passenger reported that "a rope was tossed over the rail and I put a hitch knot on it to hold it to a stanchion. As I did so, three men pushed in front of me and shoved some screaming women out of the way. They went down." Of course, many were praised for their heroic efforts. One such person was David Williamson. The twenty-seven-year-old Torontonian had finished his shift

ROPES TO SAFETY

Many escaped the flaming ship by sliding down ropes to the pier.

at Goodyear Tire at 1 a.m. and was on his way to meet friends when he heard the ten short blasts of the *Noronic*'s klaxon horn. Having worked on boats on the St. Lawrence River, Williamson recognized the international distress signal. "I saw a little flicker of fire on the back, upper deck," and ran down to the pier just as fire crews began to arrive. Pushing a nearby raft into the water, he paddled out to look for survivors. Over the next two hours Williamson dragged at least 20 passengers from the water and ferried them to shore. Others responded in similarly unselfish ways. Until they were near collapse themselves, both Police Detective Cyril Cole and Constable Robert Anderson leapt into the water countless times to pull struggling swimmers to safety.

The scene was chaotic, made worse by the screaming of passengers, the whine of ambulance and fire sirens, the shouts of rescuers and the wail of the *Noronic*'s horn stuck in the "on" position. More than 190 injured passengers were taken to Toronto hospitals and first aid centers but despite their injuries, many returned to look for loved ones, which only added to the confusion. As the number of dead grew, the Toronto morgue could not handle all the bodies and so a temporary morgue was set up at the Horticulture Building of the Canadian National Exhibition.

The ship's horn finally stopped sounding about two hours after the start of the fire and a kind of calm settled over the disaster. All those who could be saved were off the ship and firefighters spent the rest of the night aiming hoses at the smoldering wreckage. By morning, the once proud *Noronic* was just a skeleton of its former self. Every piece of wooden furniture had burned and only one staircase remained. A "sickly smell of burned bodies, hundreds of them" pervaded the area as firefighters began the gruesome task of recovering bodies. Many were so badly burned that they crumbled when touched. One firefighter, overcome with grief when he tried to move an impossibly charred body in front of the wheelhouse, leaned over the ship's rail and sobbed.

One hundred and nineteen passengers died that awful night. All of the crewmembers survived.

How and why had the *Noronic* burned? Investigators determined that the fire had started on the port side of C deck in a closet used to store maids' equipment and linens. It was hypothesized that a cigarette or faulty wiring

may have ignited the blaze. Don Church, a fire insurance specialist from Ohio, had been the first to smell the smoke coming from the locked closet and had alerted a bellboy, Ernest O'Neill, who had a key. As soon as the door opened, they were hit by thick smoke. While O'Neill searched for a fire extinguisher, Church watched helplessly as the blaze spread, fed by the new supply of oxygen. The fire extinguisher proved no match for the flames and so they ran to get a fire hose. When they aimed the nozzle, no water came out. That faulty fire hose sealed the *Noronic's* fate because at this point it is quite likely the men could have extinguished the blaze before any major damage was done. Frustrated, they went their separate ways—O'Neill to sound the alarm and Church to rouse his family.

The inquiry placed blame for the disaster with the owners of the vessel, Canada Steamship Lines, and with Captain Taylor. The investigators alleged he was drunk (which Taylor vehemently denied) and an ineffective leader during the crisis. The owners were criticized for not installing proper safety equipment and although they publicly insisted that their employees were not negligent, they were required to pay the costs of the inquiry and eventually settled more than $2 million in damage claims. Taylor's license was suspended for a year. He never returned to work on the lakes. Meanwhile, the *Noronic* was refloated and towed to Hamilton, Ontario, for scrap. Today the ship's whistle is the only artifact that remains of the once beautiful cruise ship.

VICTIMS

The next morning firefighters began removing bodies from the decks of the Noronic, *many burned beyond recognition.*

TORONTO SURPRISED
Most people in Toronto and the surrounding areas were going about their usual
Friday night activities on October 15, 1954, when Hurricane Hazel hit.

HURRICANE HAZEL

Toronto and area, Ontario

OCTOBER 15, 1954

Hurricane Hazel began her rampage in Haiti on October 12, 1954, careening over the island, destroying entire towns and leaving more than 100 dead. Continuing up the east coast of the United States, Hazel's 100 mph (160kph) winds wreaked havoc on the Carolinas, Virginia, Pennsylvania and New York before turning west towards Lake Ontario, where it came up against the Allegheny Mountains, which slowed its progress. Although an end to the path of ruin was now in sight, weather forecasters warned that the still dangerous storm would pass just east of Toronto before midnight on Friday, October 15, bringing heavy rain and winds. Because of continuous rain over the past few days, Toronto's creeks and rivers were already threatening to burst their banks. Nevertheless, most Torontonians paid little attention and continued on with their usual Friday night plans.

Joe Ward was drenched as he returned home from his job as a sheet metal worker at the De Havilland Aircraft plant. Hurrying across the wooden swing bridge that spanned the Humber River he had to slog through the gooey mess of the flooded Raymore Drive to reach his home. He and his wife Annie had saved for 15 years to buy the white and blue cottage and there were only two more mortgage payments outstanding on the property. After a dinner of fish and chips, Annie and Joe settled down in the living room in front of the television. At 9 p.m. the lights flickered out but the two were not alarmed. Annie decided to turn in for the night while Joe snoozed in his easy chair with his pet budgie on his shoulder.

Around midnight he woke up and was shocked to find the floor covered with cold water. He jumped up and waded towards the front door. Outside, the bridge he had taken home that evening had torn away from

HIGHWAY 400 UNDER WATER

Flooding on Holland Marsh washed out the highway, blocking traffic on either side.

131

HOUSE ON RAYMORE DRIVE
(Above Left) Bill Birch peers into a house. The raging Humber River carved away its banks, pulling 17 homes on Raymore Drive into the water and leaving others dangling on the shore.

BURIED IN DEBRIS
(Above Right) The rushing water was no match for many cars. One Chevrolet was swept from its garage and carried three miles (5kms) from home.

the bank, his front garden was destroyed and even more disturbing, he could hear the frightened shouts of his neighbors. He wakened Annie and grabbed a flashlight as the cottage started to tremble. They climbed onto the roof just as their home was ripped from its foundations. It seemed to fly down Raymore Drive until it came to rest against the home of Jack Anderson. Scared, Annie said to Joe, "If we die, Pop, we'll die together." For seven hours the couple clung to a television aerial and watched as the ferocious brown water came to within two feet (0.6m) of their precarious roost. They could only watch, clinging together for warmth, as other homes were uprooted and washed down the river. A helicopter rescued them at dawn, but 38 of their neighbors were not so lucky.

Elsewhere along the Humber another drama was unfolding. Gerald Elliot was driving across the Old Mill Bridge when the banks gave way. Firefighters found him clinging to the broken bridge, threw him a hose, and dragged him towards safety. However, the hose snapped in the vicious current, and Elliot was swept downstream. He managed to grasp a willow tree steadfastly rooted to the bottom about 100 feet (30m) from the bank. Harbor Police Officer Max Hurley was called around midnight to rescue the exhausted man. He gathered his lifesaving equipment and a small dinghy, and seeing that there were no trucks available to take him to the scene, commandeered a new black Cadillac parked in the Harbor Police garage. The Cadillac belonged to Dr. Bernard Willinsky, a surgeon at Mount Sinai Hospital. Jack "Hot-shot" Russell, an old friend of Hurley's, had driven Willinsky's car down to the harbor to ensure the doctor's yacht was weathering the storm. As Hurley was strapping his dinghy to the Cadillac's roof, Russell yelled,

"What the hell are you doing, Max?" Hurley shot back, "I've commandeered your Caddy for an adventure. Hop in, Hot-shot."

They arrived at the riverbank beside the washed-out bridge, where a crowd of rescuers watched helplessly as Elliot became increasingly numb with cold. Hurley immediately tied a rope around his waist and tried to pull his way along a fence rail that jutted out into the raging river. He had to be pulled back as the powerful current threatened to pull him down the river. Ropes, ladders and even a helicopter were also unsuccessful. Finally, at 3:30 a.m., Hurley took drastic action. Tying a rope to the dinghy, he and another Harbor Police officer prepared to paddle out to

the willow tree. As a test, they sent the empty boat out first. It was only 12 feet (3.6m) from the bank when it dove below the surface, sucked down by the current. It took fifteen men hauling on the rope to recover it. Refusing to give up, Hurley said, "I'm going to try to make it in the boat without a life-line... I'm going it alone. I'm a bachelor, after all." No one could stop him.

After three attempts, Hurley got the dinghy within 30 feet (9m) of Elliot. He tossed him a life jacket and yelled to jump into the stern. Elliot lunged and managed to grasp the side. "You married?" Hurley asked. "Yes. Got four kids," Elliot said through blue lips. "Well, it's a good thing your wife doesn't know where you are now," joked Hurley.

Thirty-five miles (56km) north of Toronto, on the Holland Marsh, another drama was played out. Holland Marsh was and is an area of rich farmland, owned mostly by Dutch immigrants who reclaimed the land from a swamp. The De Peuter family was not particularly alarmed by the flood warnings but around 9 p.m. sent fifteen-year-old Harry to the local store to buy extra candles. He was quite surprised to find that the doors to the

WRECKAGE
(Above) Toronto woman manages to smile for the camera while searching the wreckage for her belongings.

BODY LIFTED TO THE BLOOR STREET VIADUCT
(Below) Volunteers searched for the dead in flooded areas, mud banks and in trees.

HOLLAND MARSH

Four hundred and sixty-five families on the Holland Marsh would lose nearly everything when the marsh flooded. The circle shows a family trapped by the rising water.

CLEANING HOUSE

While some in Toronto slept through the storm and woke up to no ill effects, others faced property damages totaling over $25 million.

store were wide open and no one was there. He helped himself and turned back towards home. The only lights in the area were coming from his house. By now the water was running over the road and the wind was howling over the Marsh. The De Peuters held an impromptu family meeting and decided that with five adults and twelve children, they could not realistically leave the house to find higher ground. Before long there was two feet (0.6m) of water in the house and the family was forced upstairs. From their perch they saw dozens of floating crates of produce and then just as a neighbor's house floated by, they felt a "terrific jolt" and began moving themselves. Harry recalled, "The amazing part was all the lights in the house stayed on." From about 11:30 p.m. until 6:30 a.m. the De Peuters floated around the Marsh, finally coming to rest two miles (3.2km) from their property.

All 17 De Peuters were rescued by a brave stranger who swam out with a rope. The family didn't learn of his identity until many years later when one of the De Peuter brothers was at a paint store in Barrie, talking to the proprietor, Jack Oates. "He got to talking about the wet weather and how it wasn't as bad as Hurricane Hazel and one thing led to another and we found out that he, Jack Oates, was the man who had saved us."

The day after the hurricane, Toronto surveyed the damage. Almost 9 inches (23cm) of rain had fallen in only 48 hours. Creeks and rivers spilled over their banks and twenty bridges were washed out. Seventeen homes on Raymore Drive had been washed away; 465 families on the Holland Marsh lost everything, and 50 families were evacuated from the Pleasant Valley trailer camp when Etobicoke Creek demolished their homes. In all, 1868 families were left homeless and 81 people died in what was the most severe flood in Toronto in over 200 years.

THE AFTERMATH
(Above) The old Toronto Armoury was used to organize aid for the 1868 families left homeless.

The city went straight to work repairing the physical and emotional damage of the storm. The Red Cross and the Salvation Army housed and fed the victims while Molson Brewery's Limited Mobile Emergency Unit from Montreal gave typhoid inoculations to hundreds. Many generous citizens offered their help in unique ways. A barber offered to travel anywhere in the city to cut hair for free, a brewery volunteered to deliver milk rather than beer, a stenographer offered her typing skills and a businessman donated three cemetery plots.

As a result of the storm, the Conservation Authority in Toronto cleared the city's floodplain of residences and converted these areas into parks. Raymore Drive is now a green playground with children's swings and teeter-totters. Nothing but memories remain to tell the story of Hurricane Hazel.

JUST PIECES LEFT
*Air Canada Flight 621 en route from Montreal to Los Angeles
crashed during landing at a scheduled stopover in Toronto.*

FLIGHT 621

Air Canada DC-8-63 Crashes at Toronto Airport, Ontario

JULY 5, 1970

As Air Canada flight 621 neared the runway at Toronto International Airport just after 8 a.m. on July 5, 1970, the pilot, Peter Hamilton, and co-pilot, Donald Rowland, went through the final preparations for landing. At 60 feet (18m) from the ground, Hamilton gave a final "O.K." to Rowland and immediately after, the plane dropped sharply. The cockpit recorder captured the panic in Hamilton's voice as he shouted, "No-no-no!" The plane hit the tarmac heavily and then took off again. As the DC-8-63 left the ground, engine number 4 dropped from the wing and fell to the ground, along with a chunk of the lower wing plating. The plane climbed higher, fire and smoke trailing from the wing where fuel had escaped.

A Mrs. Day and her five-month-old daughter had started breakfast when she heard an explosion that rattled the windows in the house. She looked out to see the plane about a half-mile (0.8km) away, apparently heading right for her. "A big part fell off—it looked like the wing—and I grabbed Barbara and ran out of the house into the field, but I couldn't tell which way to run to get out of the way," said Day. The plane flew directly over her house and then crashed in a blaze of fire in a nearby field.

When the police arrived on the scene about ten minutes later, the smoldering wreckage was strewn over four hundred yards (360m). Evidence of the human cargo included burned travel bags and clothes—a stewardess' uniform hung from an oak tree. But there were no survivors to be found in the blackened mess. Investigators went about the grisly task of recovering the bodies of one hundred passengers and nine crewmembers. The ensuing inquiry showed that Rowland had deployed, rather than armed, the ground spoilers a few seconds before landing. The plane had braked in the air, which caused the sudden drop in altitude—a serious mistake seconds before landing.

MAVIS ROAD CROSSING
Twenty-three railcars derailed at the Mavis Road crossing in Mississauga, Ontario. Many were carrying deadly chemicals.

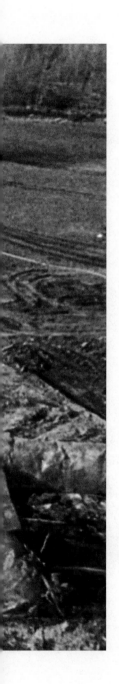

Mississauga Train Derailment

Mississauga, Ontario

November 10, 1979

Just before midnight on November 10, 1979, Canadian Pacific Freight Train No. 5 wound its way through Mississauga towards Toronto. On one of the cars, the journal box, which had not been properly lubricated, began to heat up. The resulting friction eventually caused the stub of the axle to break off, sending one set of wheels crashing into the backyard of a nearby home. Minutes later the crippled car derailed at the Mavis Road crossing, pulling 22 other cars with it. As the tankers crashed into each other, some erupted in flames. This was followed by a tremendous blast that could be heard throughout the city. Firefighters arrived to find an inferno 5000 feet (1500m) high. A second explosion knocked spectators and firefighters to the ground, and a third sent a propane tank flying through the air.

Some of the tankers were carrying deadly chemicals: chlorine, caustic soda, propane, styrene and toluene. Officials hastily called a meeting to discuss the dangers to area residents. Their main concern was the leaking chlorine tanker lying next to a burning propane tanker. If chlorine gas is inhaled it saps the fluids in the lining of a person's lungs, causing the victim to suffocate. Thirty-five hundred residents and 1400 hospital patients were quickly evacuated from the immediate area. As the wind shifted over the next few days, more residents were taken to temporary shelters. In all, over 200,000 people were evacuated.

Crews could not safely patch the chlorine tanker, which was leaking an estimated 44 to 67 pounds (20-30kg) of chlorine per hour, until the fire in the propane tanker burned out. Finally, three days after the derailment, the blaze was extinguished, but it took another three days to patch the leaking chlorine tanker. Only then could the tired but relieved residents return to their homes.

WAITING AMBULANCES

Ambulances were ready to respond but there were no casualties as a result of the Mississauga train derailment.

139

INDEX

PICTURE CREDITS

AP/Wide World Photos: 56, 104(main), 105
Archives of Ontario: 5, 74(main), 88 (main)
122(t,b), 123
Barrett, Harry and Barrett family: 88(ti,bi)
Bruce County Archives: 62(main, ti), 67, 70
Bunin, Lisa/Greenpeace: 106
Canada Steamship Lines Archives: 126(t,i)
Carlton County Historical Society: 16(b), 17
Center For Health, Environment and Justice: 108
(t,tl) (photo by Stephen Lester), 109
Chicago Historical Society: i, 39(b)
City of Toronto Archives: 120(t,i), 121(t,i)
Cleveland Optical Database, Cleveland Public
Library: 98(i)
Cleveland Picture Collection, Cleveland Public
Library: 92
Cleveland Press Collection, Cleveland State
University Library: 100
Collingwood Museum: viii, 73
Dossin Great Lakes Museum: 52(t)
Eastland Memorial Society: ix(b), 44(ti, bi), 45
Fr. Edward J. Dowling, S. J. Marine Historical
Collection, University of Detroit Mercy: 6, 26, 31,
54 (main, i), 76, 77
Frank Leslie's Illustrated Newspaper: 28, 29, 34,
39(t), 91
Great Lakes Shipwreck Historical Society, Whitefish
Point, MI: Painting by David Conklin: 17, 18
Greater Sudbury Public Library: 64, 65
Grey County Museum: 58, 59
Hamilton Public Library 116(all), 117
Historical Collections of the Great Lakes, Bowling
Green State University: 42, 66, 68, 80, 81, 96
History of Chicago, volume II, 1885: 35, 36 (all),
38 (t,b)
Jesse Besser Museum: 60
Lake Superior Marine Maritime Archives, Lake
Superior Maritime Collections, UW-Superior: 9, 8,
10, 11, 12(t,b), 13
Library of Congress: 14(i), 16(main), 46, 82, 98
Lusk, Greg, Michigan Dept. National Resources:
41

Lynx Images Inc.: 4(i), 75
Macleod, Rose. *The Story of White Cloud, Hay and
Griffith Islands*: 74(li,ri)
Mason County Historical Society: 52(b)
McGreevy, Robert, Marine Artist: 61, 86(t,b)
Metro Toronto Reference Library: 4(t), 25, 37, 44,
72, 57, 82, 84(t,b), 87, 88, 104, 110, 111, 118, 119,
124, 125(t,b), 127(t,i), 128, 129,130, 131, 133(t),
134(t)
Michigan Technological University Archives and
Copper Country Historical Collections, Michigan
Technological University: 14
Minnesota Historical Society: 53
Mississauga Public Library: 138, 139
National Archives of Canada: xi, xiii, 12, 71(tr)
Northwest Minnesota Historical Center, Duluth,
MN, McKenzie: 2, 3
Ohio Historical Society: 90(t,b)
Remmick Collection: 94(all), 95
Rindlisbacher, Peter, Marine Artist: 112, 113, 114
115(t,b)
Robinson, Gregory: 7
Seawolf Communications, Cris Kohl: 69(t), 71(tl,b)
State Archives of Michigan: 40
State Construction Safety Commission: 79
Stonehouse, Frederick: 47, 48, 49(all), 50, 51
Sullivan, Richard and Avery Color Studios: 21(t)
Thunder Bay Historical Museum Society: ix(b), 4(b)
Toronto Star, B. Spremo, C.M.: 134 (b), 136
Toronto Telegram: 132(r,l) 133(b), 135
Tyler, John A.: 94(ti,b)
The Times Herald, Port Huron, MI: 78
U.S. Coast Guard: 20(b), 21(i)
The Windsor Star: 102(all), 103
Wisconsin Maritime Museum: 24
Wisconsin Historical Society (Iconographic
Collection: vi, vii, 22, 23, 32

ACKNOWLEDGEMENTS

This book could not have been written without the generous assistance of the following individuals and organizations. Any errors or omissions in the text, however, are mine alone.

American Society of Civil Engineering, Research Library
Charles A. Burnham, Executive Chairman, Ashtabula Railway Historical Foundation
Lynn M. Duchez Bycko, Digital Production Unit, Special Collections, Cleveland State University Library
Bob Carroll, Picture Editor and Rob Gurdebeke, Assistant Photo Editor, *The Windsor Star*
Cleveland Public Library Photograph Collection
Lisa Cotton, Occidental Chemical Corporation
Matthew L. Daley, University Archivist, University of Detroit Mercy Libraries/Media Services, Special Collections/ Fr. Edward J. Dowling Marine Historical Collection
Mr. Neil Durbin, Media Relations Representative, Dominion Gas
T. J. Gaffney, Curator of Collections, Port Huron Museum
Neil Garneau, Collections Coordinator, Owen Sound Marine & Rail Museum
Robert W. Graham, Archivist, Historical Collections of the Great Lakes, Bowling Green State University
Grey County Museum
Lesley Hammond, Reference Department, Bay City Branch Library
Richard Haynes, Historic Fort York
Dee Anna Grimsrud, Reference Archivist, Wisconsin Historical Society
Max Hanley
Jerry Hilliker
Sean Ley, Great Lakes Shipwreck Historical Society
Laura Lombardi, Greenpeace
Greg Lusk, Greg Lusk Collection
Patricia Maus, Manager/Curator of Manuscripts, Northeast Minnesota Historical Center
Robert McGreevey, Marine Artist
Nada Mehes and Bernard E. Lemieux, Greater Sudbury Public Library
Minnesota Historical Society Library
Robert A. Murnan, Cleveland Research Center
Ohio Historical Society
Peter Rindlisbacher
Remmick Collection
Frederick Stonehouse
Merrit Strum
Karl Sup, Eastland Memorial Society
Lisa Watson, Air Canada
Marlene Wisuri, Carlton County Historical Society
Ron Wood, Mason County Historical Society

Special thanks to Janet Looker whose book, *Disaster Canada*, has proven an invaluable resource.

I owe an extraordinary debt of gratitude to the partners of Lynx Images Inc. for entrusting me with this project. Thanks to Russell Floren for the numerous opportunities and exceptional project producing, Barbara J. Chisholm for helpful advice along the way, and Andrea Gutsche for her distinct design and assistance with gathering the pictures. I am also extremely grateful for Barbara D. Chisholm's succinct editing, Amy Harkness' excellent copy editing and proofreading, and Steve Gamester's initial research.

SELECTED BIBLIOGRAPHY

Barry, James P. *Ships of the Great Lakes: 300 Years of Navigation.* Berkeley: Howell-North Books, 1973.

Barry, James P. *Wrecks and Rescues of the Great Lakes: A Photographic History.* Lansing, MI: Thunder Bay Press, 1994.

Bourrie, Mark. *Ninety Fathoms Down: Canadian Stories of the Great Lakes.* Toronto: Hounslow Press, 1995.

Boyer, Dwight. *Ghost Ships of the Great Lakes.* New York: Dodd, Mead, 1968.

Boyer, Dwight. *True Tales of the Great Lakes.* New York: Dodd, Mead, 1971.

Cahill, Jack. *Hot Box: the Mississauga Miracle.* Markham, Ont.: Paperjacks, 1980.

Cain, Emily. *Ghost Ships—Hamilton & Scourge: Historical Treasures from the War of 1812.* Toronto: Musson, Beaufort Books, 1983.

Carroll, Francis M. & Franklin R. Raiter. *The Fires of Autumn: The Cloquet-Moose Lake Disaster of 1918.* Minnesota: Minnesota Historical Society Press, 1990.

Cowan, David. *Great Chicago Fires: Historic Blazes That Shaped a City.* Chicago: Lake Claremont Press, 2001.

Craig, John. *The Noronic is Burning!* Don Mills, Ontario: General Publishing Co. Limited, 1976.

Davis, Lee. *Environmental Disasters: A Chronicle of Individual, Industrial, and Governmental Carelessness.* New York: Facts on File, 1998.

Dedmon, Emmett. *Fabulous Chicago.* New York: Atheneum, 1981.

Gibbs, Lois Marie. *Love Canal: My Story.* Albany: State University of New York Press, 1982.

Gibbs, Lois Marie. *Love Canal: The Story Continues.* Gabriola Island, B.C.: New Society Publishers, 1998.

Floren, Russell & Andrea Gutsche. *Ghosts of the Bay: A Guide to the History of Georgian Bay.* Toronto: Lynx Images Inc., 1994.

Graham, Paul. *Disaster! Canadian Catastrophes: Natural and Man-made.* Toronto: Canadian Reinsurance Co., 1992.

Gutsche, Andrea & Cindy Bisaillon. *Mysterious Islands: Forgotten Tales of the Great Lakes.* Toronto: Lynx Images Inc., 1999.

Gutsche, Andrea, Barbara Chisholm & Russell Floren. *The North Channel and St. Mary's River: A Guide to the History.* Toronto: Lynx Images Inc., 1997.

Gutsche, Andrea, Barbara Chisholm & Russell Floren. *Alone in the Night: Lighthouses of Georgian Bay, Manitoulin Island and the North Channel.* Toronto: Lynx Images Inc., 1996.

Halliday, Hugh A. *Wreck! Canada's Worst Railway Accidents.* Toronto: Robin Brass Studio, 1997.

Havey, Mary Claire. *Derailment: The Mississauga Miracle.* Toronto: Government of Ontario, 1980.